What People Are Saying about Don Gossett's Ministry and Writings...

I was first introduced to the ministry of Don Gossett in 1976 while in Bible college. His book, *The Power of Your Words,* made such an impact on my life that I have ordered hundreds of them over the years to give away.

Don is truly a modern-day hero of faith, and my church enthusiastically supports his world evangelism. Don's wisdom, experience, and revelation have been some of the greatest blessings in my life.

Pastor Glen Curry
Pillars of Faith Christian Center
Industry, California

We became acquainted with Don Gossett's ministry in the late '70s when we began listening to the *Bold Bible Living* radio program, reading his many books, and supporting his ministry. His teachings from the Word have truly revolutionized and shaped our lives and ministry. The victories and successes we have experienced are largely attributed to his impact on our lives. Don Gossett is truly a spiritual father and a friend to us, and we are eternally grateful to him.

Pastor Jim and Rosie Parker
Living Word Christian Center
Spokane, Washington

Each of Don Gossett's books, which God placed into my hands, helped me to advance one step further in my divine destiny. The benefits have been so great that whenever this man of God speaks, I listen. Whenever this man of God writes, I read....

Whether it is through the pages of his books, or in person, Don Gossett has an anointing to stir up and enlarge people's lives. My life is one testimony of his powerful and transforming ministry.

Senior Pastor Dr. Roge Abergel
World Harvest Church
Van Nuys, California

Don Gossett has blessed the Christian world for over fifty years with his dynamic, faith-filled message of Jesus Christ's complete salvation, deliverance, and healing. This book, like his previous writings, will ignite the spark of faith within us to trust Jesus for all of our needs.

Reverend Dr. Jerry Lynn
Reach Out Fellowship
Albany, New York

Don Gossett's walk with God has been a remarkable journey that will inspire faith in all who hear him in person or read his anointed writings. He is gifted in his ability to communicate the benefits of confessing the Word of God.

Pastor Holmes Williams, D.D.
The People's Cathedral
Barbados

THE POWER OF
SPOKEN FAITH

THE POWER OF
SPOKEN
FAITH

DON GOSSETT
E. W. KENYON

W

WHITAKER
HOUSE

Unless otherwise indicated, all Scripture quotations are taken from the King James Version (KJV) of the Bible.
Scripture quotations marked (NIV) are from the Holy Bible, New International Version, © 1973, 1978, 1984 by the International Bible Society. Used by permission.
Quotations marked (MESSAGE) are taken from *The Message* by Eugene H. Peterson, © 1993, 1994, 1995, 1996. Used by permission of the NavPress Publishing Group. All rights reserved.
Scripture quotations marked (NKJV) are from the *New King James Version*, © 1979, 1980, 1982 by Thomas Nelson, Inc. Used by permission. All rights reserved.

THE POWER OF SPOKEN FAITH

Don Gossett
P. O. Box 2
Blaine, Washington 98231
website: www.dongossett.com

ISBN: 0-88368-675-9
Printed in the United States of America
© 2003 by Don Gossett

Whitaker House
30 Hunt Valley Circle
New Kensington, PA 15068
website: www.whitakerhouse.com

Library of Congress Cataloging-in-Publication Data

Gossett, Don, 1929–
  The power of spoken faith / Don Gossett and E. W. Kenyon.
    p. cm.
  ISBN 0-88368-675-9 (pbk.)
  1. Christian life. 2. Oral communication—Religious
aspects—Christianity. I. Kenyon, Essek William, 1867–1948.
II. Title.
  BV4597.53.C64 G67 2001
  248.4–dc21
                                              2001004379

    1 2 3 4 5 6 7 8 9 10 11 / 10 09 08 07 06 05 04 03

Acknowledgments

Let me introduce you to several people who exemplify the true spirit of generosity.

First and foremost is Dr. E. W. Kenyon. It was the passion of his life to share with others what God had taught him through the Word. He diligently applied himself to writing sixteen books, editing hundreds of magazines, and creating Bible study courses and gospel tracts. What a giving heart he demonstrated!

Second, before Dr. Kenyon passed away in 1948, he asked his daughter, Ruth, to keep the work going. For fifty years, Ruth was faithful to do so. Many times she shared with me how fulfilling it was to see and know the effectiveness of her father's writings—literally all over the globe.

Next, I am pleased to commend the excellent work of Pastor Joe McIntyre, who now serves as president of Kenyon's Gospel Publishing Society.

When books were published presenting "unfair and unscholarly" attacks on the writings of Dr. Kenyon, Joe felt compelled to write an apologetic thesis, which he presented to his church family.

I admire Joe McIntyre for his labor of love in investing hundreds of hours of research and authoring the book, *E. W. Kenyon and His Message of Faith: The True Story.*

Last, Charisma House, owned by my dear friend, Stephen Strang, generously gave me permission to include materials from Pastor McIntyre's aforementioned book here in *The Power of Spoken Faith.*

My special thanks go to Dr. T. L. Osborn, Tulsa, Oklahoma, for his contributions toward this book.

I also owe my appreciation to Pastor Don Cox, Waterloo, Iowa, for items he has shared with me.

—Don Gossett

Contents

⌁ Part III: The Fruits of Spoken Faith ⌁

Foreword

Pastor George Hunter was a close associate of Dr. E. W. Kenyon and most likely the author of the following tribute, written in November of 1930. He knew firsthand the triumphs and trials of Kenyon's life, and his words are freighted with love and caring. His message touched my heart. I pray it will likewise minister to you.

—Don Gossett

Mountains and Valleys

No man that we know of has such a gift as a teacher. We all wonder at him, but let us remember the price he has had to pay.

I have seen Dr. Kenyon suffer as few men have suffered.

During those early days at the Bible school, the things I saw him pass through are almost unbelievable. I saw him suffer persecution from brethren. I remember the early struggles against false teachings. I saw him suffer financial loss and misunderstanding. I saw the work of false friends. I saw those he helped, turn traitor. I knew of heartaches unknown to the crowds. Then I saw sickness and death come and take his mate [she died in 1914]. I stood at the graveside with him. I saw men rob him of all he had labored for. Lies, abuse, and insults were heaped upon him, and in the midst of it all he walked like a king, and God gave him victory in his soul.

I have also seen him enjoy happy days and prosperity, without losing his head.

I remember the high spots in his life—when a great Bible school was in full swing; when evangelistic tours were winning thousands; when the country was praising him; when he again took a bride to himself and had a happy home; when he enjoyed the love of a great body of young ministers whom he had trained.

Mountains and valleys, one after another, have all worked together to make the teacher what he is today.

The text from *Mountains and Valleys* is taken from a Figueroa Independent Baptist Church bulletin (1930), as quoted in *E. W. Kenyon and His Message of Faith: The True Story* by Joe McIntyre (Lake Mary, FL: Charisma House, 1997), 153–154.

Introduction

*It is written: "I believed; therefore I have
spoken." With that same spirit of faith
we also believe and therefore speak.*
—2 Corinthians 4:13 NIV

In 1952, I was given a copy of *The Wonderful
Name of Jesus*, by Dr. E. W. Kenyon. My study
of this book was enhanced by the fact that
just the year before, at an altar of prayer, I had
received a startling revelation of the authority of
the name of Jesus. This came from Philippians
2:9–11:

> *Wherefore God also hath highly exalted him,
> and given him a name which is above every
> name: that at the name of Jesus every knee
> should bow, of things in heaven, and things in
> earth, and things under the earth; and that
> every tongue should confess that Jesus Christ is
> Lord, to the glory of God the Father.*

Dr. Kenyon's revelation of the name of Jesus set my soul on fire. I was ministering in tent meetings in Fresno and Modesto, California, at that time. I did daily early morning radio broadcasts on stations in Lodi and Modesto. Driving from each city, I was flowing in an enormous appreciation of the majesty of the name. Over and over, I sang songs and choruses about the precious name.

I was then able to make contact with Ruth Kenyon, Dr. Kenyon's daughter and head of Kenyon's Gospel Publishing Society.

In my first phone conversation with Ruth, she informed me that Dr. Kenyon had left sixteen books to posterity, which she ordered for me. She also explained that Dr. Kenyon's *In His Presence* was the book God was using most at that time.

When I received the shipment of Dr. Kenyon's sixteen books, I eagerly studied and devoured them all. Knowing the blessing *The Wonderful Name* had been to me there in California, I expected *In His Presence* would likewise ignite my heart.

However, my first reading of the book didn't achieve that for me. A few months later, while in meetings in Kansas City, I reread *In His Presence*. That time, the revelation came to my spirit. I was so caught up in His presence that I felt I was walking on fleecy clouds as I went from my hotel to the church where I was ministering.

I then realized that it was necessary for the Holy Spirit to give me revelation knowledge to grasp what Dr. Kenyon had written.

In my youthful zeal, I once said to my friends, "I so love what the Kenyon books have done for me, I think I would almost like to change my name to 'Don Kenyon,' so I could be readily identified with his wonderful ministry." (Of course, I didn't make that change. I'm still Don Gossett.)

In 1954, I was back in Southern California for meetings. At that time, the Kenyon's Gospel Publishing Society offices were in Fullerton, not far from Los Angeles where I was ministering. One day, I made an appointment to drive out to Fullerton and meet with Ruth and her mother.

It was an unforgettable experience. I asked Ruth, "I have been an avid reader and student of many books written by evangelical and Pentecostal authors. Why is it your father had the ability to open the Word with such unique authority?"

Ruth replied, "Don, if you had grown up in my father's house, perhaps you would understand. The open Bible was all over our home.

"One of the sweetest experiences in my youth was passing by our bathroom where my father would often shave with the door ajar. He would be dressed except for his shirt. His face would be lathered to prepare for his shave. But beside the sink would be an open Bible. He couldn't keep his eyes off the Word. I would hear him rejoicing, weeping, and praising God for some nugget of truth he had read in the Scriptures."

A few years later, Ruth moved the Kenyon's Gospel Publishing Society offices back to Lynnwood, Washington, less than a hundred miles from my home in Surrey. She invited me to be a regular contributor to *Kenyon's Herald of Life,* a paper she published.

After Ruth's husband, Mr. Iams, passed away, I wrote an article entitled "Again She Stands Alone." I emphasized how Dr. Kenyon had selected Ruth to continue his ministry the very day he knew the Lord was calling him home. Dr. Kenyon's wife had joined Ruth in the ministry until the Lord called her home also. Now, with her mother and father already gone, Mr. Iams' passing left Ruth alone.

The Reverend Norman Houseworth, in northern Alberta, Canada, read the article I wrote. His wife had died a few years before, and the Lord used my article to give him a nudge. He went to meet Ruth with the prospect of their being married, and that is exactly what happened.

In 1972, I requested and was given Ruth's permission to use Kenyon's writings in my book, *The Power of Your Words*.* The book was about the confession of the Word and combined Dr. Keyon's excellent materials on the subject with my own recorded thoughts.

When Ruth went to be with the Lord a few years ago, the Kenyon staff gave Joe McIntyre access to writings of Dr. Kenyon that had never been released. Pastor McIntyre did excellent research and wrote his book, *E. W. Kenyon and His Message of Faith: The True Story.* I have included quotations and items from Joe McIntyre's book in this book, *The Power of Spoken Faith.*

The Power of Spoken Faith carries the same format as *The Power of Your Words*. The author of each chapter is identified either by the initials "EWK," for Dr. E. W. Kenyon, or "DEG," for myself.

It is my prayer that this book will bless you and encourage you to realize the power of your spoken faith.

---

* This book is also available through Whitaker House.

Part I

Principles of Affirmation

Reaching and Touching
in Faith

|DEG|

Reaching out in faith results in the most significant touch of all—the touch of God. In October of 1960, my family and I moved from Tulsa, Oklahoma, to Vancouver, British Columbia, to begin a new ministry. For a year, we traveled the Canadian prairies, conducting evangelistic meetings in churches. For those twelve months, we journeyed without having a place to really call home.

My five children recall that period of time as one of the most adventurous seasons of their lives, but it wasn't easy for them. Michael and

Judy slept on the back seat of our old 1956 Buick. Jeanne and Donnie slept on the floorboard. Our baby, Marisa, slept between Joyce and me in the front seat.

Having gotten a "lemon" in business matters (one that cost us the home we had owned), by the grace of God we made lemonade.

During those months, I taught my children to memorize many verses of God's Word, and all of them delighted in the Bible stories I taught them. Michael says he memorized more than one hundred Bible verses during that time.

We enrolled the children who were school-age in the British Columbia Correspondence School, and my wife, Joyce, taught them while we were on the road.

In 1961, we decided to settle in a little motel unit in Victoria so that we could put our children in school. Things didn't go especially well with all seven of us living in two rooms. Cramped is an appropriate word to describe this time in our lives.

For five weeks of that fall, I conducted meetings in a church in Longview, Washington, with Pastor Jim Nichols. I received a love offering for my ministry each week. But while there was lots of love, there just wasn't much offering. One Monday, I had serious car trouble on the way home and had to use most of my love offering to get my car repaired. There wasn't enough left over to pay the thirty dollars necessary for the rental of our little motel unit.

The embarrassment of not being able to pay the rent, plus inadequate clothes and provisions for my children, was nearly more than I could take.

I made arrangements to postpone paying the rent for a week, left Joyce what money I had for the week's groceries, and returned to my meetings in Longview.

To walk with God, you must agree with God.

I asked God many questions. "Why are we in such desperate need financially?" "Why did we lose our home by repossession?"

During that time, I read a wonderful book called *Word Power*, by Vernon Howard. God used the message of that book to help me freshly understand the power of my words, and He gave me this Scripture: *"Can two walk together, except they be agreed?"* (Amos 3:3). God was asking me, "Do you want to walk with Me? Then you must agree with Me. You agree with Me by saying what My Word says. You have disagreed with Me by speaking lack, sickness, fear, defeat, and inability. If you want to walk with Me, you must agree with Me." As this truth became real to me, I asked His forgiveness for my failure to agree with Him and His Word.

I must not hasten away from the truth of Amos 3:3. It's in the heart of all sincere Christians to walk closely with the Lord. The Bible records the testimony of Enoch: "[He] *walked with God*" (Genesis 5:24). Enoch isn't the only person who could walk with God; you and I can also walk with Him. Hebrews 11:5 says that Enoch *"pleased God"* by agreeing in faith with God. We can walk just as closely to God as Enoch did if we choose to agree with Him in faith.

How do we agree with God? We agree by saying what God says while disagreeing with the wicked, lying Devil. (Hallelujah for such a dynamic truth!)

As a result of this realization, I began to agree with God as I had never done before. The Holy Spirit began teaching me some key Scriptures: *"Ye have wearied the Lord with your words. Yet ye say, Wherein have we wearied him?"* (Malachi 2:17).

God put His finger on the ways I had wearied Him with my words—expressing my worries and frustrations concerning my "lack of money." *"Your words have been stout against me, saith the LORD. Yet ye say, What have we spoken so much against thee?"* (Malachi 3:13).

I cried out in protest, "Lord, I would never speak against You! I love You with all my heart. Oh, Lord, I would never, never speak against You!"

Tenderly, the Lord dealt with me. *"'Your words have been stout.'* They have been strong and defensive against Me because they have been out of harmony with My Word. You have spoken words far below the standard of My Word. You must discipline your lips so that our words will be in harmony."

As I meditated on this unusual encounter with the living God, I wrote down twelve affirmations that were to become my daily discipline. I called this list of affirmations "My Never Again List."

People have often asked me, "Why did you write this list?" I wrote it as a desperate man, seeking God's ways to overcome all the adversities, financial failures, defeats, and bondages I had known for some time. I didn't write it to impress anyone with my writing ability. It was written as a discipline of my own heart in order to let the Word of God prevail as Acts 19:20 says, *"So mightily grew the word of God and prevailed."*

These twelve affirmations became the watchwords of my new walk with God. They became the grade card by which to check my life. God's Word in these twelve affirmations became the solid ground I stood on. They were the anchor that prevented me from sinking in a sea of failure, fear, and satanic oppressions.

God's Word can become an anchor.

I could use many words to describe the impact these twelve affirmations have had on my life—words like "awesome" and "life-changing." When I wrote "My Never Again List," I wasn't thinking of the millions of people who would eventually read this powerful discipline and experience their own transformations. I wrote it as a step in my pursuit of God.

Jesus declared that we are His disciples; a disciple is someone who disciplines himself. This list of affirmations has never been a magic formula; instead, it is a clear-cut discipline. It is putting Amos 3:3 into practice and agreeing with God in all areas of life.

I will always praise God for directing me to write down this list of affirmations. If no one else had been blessed by it, I would still praise the Lord. But, in addition to its blessing to me, it has been printed in many languages and distributed throughout the world. God has used it to minister to literally millions of people, people who have read it and put it into practice.

The list is founded on Romans 10:8–10:

But what saith it? The word is nigh thee, even in thy mouth, and in thy heart: that is, the word of faith, which we preach; that if thou shalt confess with thy mouth the Lord Jesus, and shalt believe in thine heart that God hath raised him from the dead, thou shalt be saved. For with the heart man believeth unto righteousness; and with the mouth confession is made unto salvation.

It is also in harmony with the spirit of faith as revealed in 2 Corinthians 4:13:

We having the same spirit of faith, according as it is written, I believed, and therefore have I spoken; we also believe, and therefore speak.

"My Never Again List"

୶ Never again will I confess I can't, for *"I can do all things through Christ which strengtheneth me"* (Philippians 4:13).

୶ Never again will I confess lack, for *"my God shall supply all* [my] *need according to his riches in glory by Christ Jesus"* (Philippians 4:19).

୶ Never again will I confess fear, for *"God hath not given us the spirit of fear; but of power, and of love, and of a sound mind"* (2 Timothy 1:7).

∽ Never again will I confess doubt and lack of faith, for *"God hath dealt to every man the measure of faith"* (Romans 12:3).

∽ Never again will I confess weakness, for *"the Lord is the strength of my life"* (Psalm 27:1), and, *"the people that do know their God shall be strong, and do exploits"* (Daniel 11:32).

∽ Never again will I confess supremacy of Satan over my life, *"because greater is he that is in* [me], *than he that is in the world"* (1 John 4:4).

∽ Never again will I confess defeat, for *"God... always causeth us to triumph in Christ"* (2 Corinthians 2:14).

∽ Never again will I confess lack of wisdom, for *"Christ Jesus...has become for us wisdom from God"* (1 Corinthians 1:30 NIV).

∽ Never again will I confess the domination of sickness over my life, for *"with his stripes we are healed"* (Isaiah 53:5).

∽ Never again will I confess worries and frustrations, for I am *"casting all* [my] *care upon him; for he careth for* [me]*"* (1 Peter 5:7). In Christ I am "care free."

∽ Never again will I confess bondage, for Scripture says, *"Where the Spirit of the Lord is, there is liberty"* (2 Corinthians 3:17). My body is the temple of the Holy Spirit.

ᔓ Never again will I confess condemnation, for *"there is therefore now no condemnation to them which are in Christ Jesus"* (Romans 8:1). I am in Christ; therefore I am free from condemnation.

That We Might
Be Healed

| EWK |

I saw the first miracles of healing in my ministry in [the Free Baptist Church at] Springville,
New York, where I was pastor.

Before this I had always been suspicious of
anyone who claimed their prayers [for healing]
were answered....I felt we had doctors and sur-
geons and sanitariums for that purpose. Why did
we need anything else? [At the time, I] firmly
believed that God had given us physicians and
other methods of healing.

I knew nothing about the name of Jesus [or]
that healing was part of the plan of redemption,

but my heart was very hungry and I was studying the Word diligently. I had just received the Holy Spirit. The Word had become a living thing. I had awakened faith in many hearts by my newfound love for the Word.

One day, the clerk of our church...asked me if I would pray for his wife. She had been ill for many months. I will never forget how I shrank from it. [But] I had to go. She lay in bed, and I prayed for her the best I knew how. I did not understand about the name of Jesus, but God in His great grace honored me and she was instantly healed. That night she came to church and gave her testimony. It created a great deal of sensation and some criticism. Some said it was her time to get well anyway. A few gave credit where it belonged.

The Word had become a living thing.

A young woman in a neighboring town was healed next. She was helpless, unable to walk. If I remember correctly, she had had an operation and it had left her in a fearful condition. I prayed for her. She was instantly healed and got up and went about her work. She is now on our correspondence list.

From that day on healings came—not many, for not many people asked to be prayed for. While we were holding services in Massachusetts, healings became more frequent. One day I discovered the use of the name of Jesus. Then miracles became a daily occurrence.

In our work at the Tabernacle, I did not teach healing except in a very guarded way. Yet as the people began to obey the Word and to test its promises, healings and other signs followed, and I could not suppress the truth. Had I any right to hold down the truth through fear of persecution or misrepresentation when I knew that God could heal, and was healing, the sick?

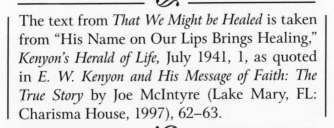

The text from *That We Might be Healed* is taken from "His Name on Our Lips Brings Healing," *Kenyon's Herald of Life,* July 1941, 1, as quoted in *E. W. Kenyon and His Message of Faith: The True Story* by Joe McIntyre (Lake Mary, FL: Charisma House, 1997), 62–63.

Daily Affirmations

|DEG|

To affirm is to make firm. An affirmation is a statement of truth you make firm by repetition. *"These things...affirm constantly"* (Titus 3:8). *"Let us hold unswervingly to the hope we profess, for he who promised is faithful"* (Hebrews 10:23 NIV). Your faith becomes effective by acknowledging every good thing that is in you in Christ Jesus. (See Philemon 6.)

The Bible has hundreds of passages that speak about about the power of words. I challenge you to speak the twenty-five affirmations that I have listed. They will be more effective as you speak them with volume, feeling, conviction, and enthusiasm. Words weakly spoken have minimal results.

I encourage you to speak some of these affirmations three to five times daily. Jesus is our primary example of how to live the Christian life, and in Matthew 26:44, "[Jesus] *prayed the third time, saying the same words.*"

Speak aloud the following affirmations during the first hour of your day:

∽ *"This is the day the Lord has made; let us rejoice and be glad in it."*   (Psalm 118:24 NIV)

∽ Today I choose love instead of fear. I choose peace instead of conflict. I choose to be a love-finder instead of a faultfinder. I choose to be a love-giver instead of a love-seeker.

∽ *"I will bless the Lord at all times: his praise shall continually be in my mouth."*   (Psalm 34:1)

∽ *"Let the weak say, I am strong"* (Joel 3:10). (Notice that it's the weak, not the strong, who are commanded to affirm this!)

∽ I am a woman/man of God. He has cleansed me by the blood of Christ. My Father has filled me with His Spirit. So I am dedicated to the Lord Jesus, strong and powerful in Him. I worship and serve Him with all the divine energy He inspires within me.

∽ *"Greater is he that is in* [me]*, than he that is in the world."*   (1 John 4:4)

༷ I am humble, strong, courageous, full of faith and powerful in the Lord. (Repeat three times.)

༷ *"If God be for us, who can be against us?"*
(Romans 8:31)

༷ I am a child of God. My Father has adopted me into His family. He has moved me out of darkness and into the light of His kingdom. God's protective shield is about me, and He is providing for every need in my life.

༷ *"My God shall supply all* [my] *need according to his riches in glory by Christ Jesus."*
(Philippians 4:19)

The Lord is the strength of my life.

༷ Every day in every way, by the grace of God, I am getting better and better through a positive attitude, spoken words of faith, and disciplined actions.

༷ *"God has not given us a spirit of fear; but of power, and of love, and of a sound mind."*
(2 Timothy 1:7 NKJV)

༷ God has forgiven me, and I forgive myself.

༷ The anointing of the Holy One abides within me. (See 1 John 2:27.)

∽ My generous Father has blessed me with abundant life. I am grateful for this, and I enjoy giving my time, talents, money, and love to others.

∽ *"But he was wounded for our transgressions, he was bruised for our iniquities: the chastisement of our peace was upon him; and with his stripes we are healed."*   (Isaiah 53:5)

∽ God loves me with an unconditional love, so I love Him with all my heart, soul, and mind. I am free to love myself, and this allows me to love my neighbor.

∽ [We overcome] *him by the blood of the Lamb and by the word of* [our] *testimony;* [we do] *not love* [our] *lives so much as to shrink from death."*
                    (Revelation 12:11 NKJV)

∽ I belong to Jesus, so I am friendly, strong, happy, and victorious. Everything is fine.

∽ *"Rejoice in the Lord alway: and again I say, Rejoice."*   (Philippians 4:4)

∽ God has given me a strong body, a fine brain, and has filled me with His Holy Spirit. This makes me a talented, gifted, persistent, and hard worker. I will reach my goals.

∽ *"The Lord is the strength of my life; of whom shall I be afraid?"*   (Psalm 27:1)

- God loves me, so I love Him, believe in Him, and trust my life to His care. I will faithfully serve Him!

- I *"cast all* [my] *anxiety on him because he cares for* [me]" (1 Peter 5:7 NIV).

- I feel healthy; I feel happy—I feel terrific! *"The Lord is the strength of my life"* (Psalm 27:1).

- God is my loving Father. He has given me a Savior, His Holy Spirit, a healthy body, a fine mind, material abundance, a beautiful world, and many friends. I am thankful! I am thankful! I am thankful!

The Power of Affirmations

|EWK|

I once doubted the efficacy of affirmations, but when I read in the first five books of Moses the expression "I am Jehovah" occuring more than twenty-five hundred times, then I knew the value of affirming, reiterating, [and] confessing the fullness of Jesus Christ and of His finished work in the presence of my weakness; in the presence of my enemies; in the presence of hell.

I would suggest that the reader constantly affirm to his own soul the great outstanding facts of redemption. They may not mean much the first time you repeat them, but...constantly reaffirm them. By and by, the Spirit will illumine them and your soul will be flooded with light and joy.

Every time I repeat what God has said about the church, about Himself, and about me as an individual, these truths reach down deep into my inner being with strength and joy and victory.

Continual affirmation has infinite value.

Only recently have I seen with clearness the infinite value of continually affirming, not only to our inner man, our own soul and spirit, but to the world. Our spiritual life depends upon our constantly affirming what God has declared, what God is in Christ, and what we are before the Father in Christ.

The thing that made Methodism so mighty in its early days was a continual confession of the things for which Mr. Wesley stood. When they stopped affirming, faith stopped growing, and believing or acting upon the Word became more and more difficult.

Maintain Your Testimony

I can remember when I dared not confess what God says I am. And my faith [sank] to the level of my confession.

If I dared not say I was the righteousness of God, Satan took advantage of my confession.

If I dared not say that my body was perfectly well and that Satan had no dominion over it, disease and pain followed my negation.

Since I have learned to know Him and to know His redemptive ability, and to know our ability in Christ, I have been able to maintain a testimony, a confession of the completeness of the finished work of Christ, of the utter reality of the new birth.

The text from *The Power of Affirmations* is taken from "Dare You Confess That You Are What God Says You Are?" *Kenyon's Herald of Life,* July 1941, 2; "The Potency of Affirming What God Says," *Living Messages,* February 1930, 30; and "Confession," *Living Messages,* April 1930, 45, as quoted in *E. W. Kenyon and His Message of Faith: The True Story* by Joe McIntyre (Lake Mary, FL: Charisma House, 1997), 260–262.

The Believing Heart and the Confessing Mouth

| EWK |

Confession, or testimony, holds a larger place in the drama of redemption than the church has ever given it. When the Word tells us to *"hold fast our confession"* [Hebrews 4:14 NKJV], it means that we are to hold fast to our testimony of what God is to us, what He has done for us, what He has done in the past, and what He is doing in us now....

If the Lord heals you, you must tell it; if the Lord heals your spirit, heals your mind, heals your body, you must tell it. Go home and tell what wondrous things the Lord has wrought. If you are afraid to tell it...you will lose the blessing that belongs to you. If men can frighten you so you will not give your testimony, in a little while you will have no testimony to give. Public confession, or giving your testimony, and faith are so closely related that if you lose your testimony... your faith will die out immediately. You keep your testimony clear by continuously giving [it] wisely in the spirit, and your faith will grow by leaps and bounds.

Boldness in Testimony

How often we sit in prayer meetings and listen to people giving what is called a testimony when they are not witnessing of Christ. They are witnessing of their own doubts and fears, or perhaps their own fancies or some hobby, rather than witnessing [to] the saving power of the work of Christ and...the joy they have in communion and fellowship with the Father through the Spirit.

Just a word in regard to testifying—the very word *testify* gives us an inkling. We are on the witness stand and are going to say something that will glorify our Lord; we want to win the case for Him. We want the unsaved people [who] hear to accept Him as their Savior, and we desire that the words that we speak shall encourage weaker believers to abandon themselves more entirely to His care.

I cannot believe that we should testify because it is our duty, but our witness should flow from a heart filled with a desire to do it because He has been so good to us.

We should not eulogize ourselves, but Him of whom we witness.

———— ✍ ————

Tell what wondrous things the Lord has wrought.

———— ✍ ————

I was in a meeting recently where the young converts testified. One after another, [they rose] with Bibles or New Testaments in hand and read some appropriate verse in connection with the subject on which the leader had spoken, and then as they wove their witness, testimony, or experience around [those] words, it left a very inspiring impression.

The Lord has had an opportunity to work through His own Word and the workers have given their testimony and experience and have also sent forth the Word that "shall not return unto Him void" [Isaiah 55:11].

Developing Spiritual Power

Yes, we must witness for Him first with our lives, but we must witness for Him with our mouths as well, for *"with the mouth confession is made unto salvation"* [Romans 10:10] and *"whosoever...shall confess me before men, him will I confess also before my Father which is in heaven"* [Matthew 10:32].

If you want to develop the spiritual power that is within you, speak out what you have to say....It will do you more good to give a stumbling, halting testimony that is all your own than to read the most flowery thing ever written by any other man....People wish to hear real testimonies from the children of God who are on fire for Him....

People say of me that I am all right until I get to talking about my friends, and then they say I am apt to become a little enthusiastic. Get into that spirit in regard to your Father and your Savior and you will never have any trouble giving a testimony that is your own, one that is alive and to which men and God will listen.

God wants us to witness in our daily life with men, telling them how good and real He is to us....He desires us, through a simple confession in prayer meetings, to say we are Christians. He wishes to be highly spoken of. He wants us to magnify Him in our testimony.

The text from *The Believing Heart and the Confessing Mouth* is taken from "Testifying or Witnessing," *Reality,* December 1904, 44–45, as quoted in *E. W. Kenyon and His Message of Faith: The True Story* by Joe McIntyre (Lake Mary, FL: Charisma House, 1997), 51, 246–247.

The Power of
Spoken Words

|DEG|

I have put my fingers in the ears of hundreds of people who were totally deaf. Many of them didn't even have eardrums. Putting my fingers in those ears, I have spoken the words, "In the name of Jesus, I command the spirits of deafness to leave these ears. In Jesus' mighty name, I command the hearing to come in strong and normal."

The results have been miraculous. Most of the people have been completely healed so that they can hear even the faintest whispering or the ticking of a tiny wristwatch!

It overwhelms me when I consider the wonder of it! Just by the words of authority, in the name of Jesus, creative miracles can take place. Physical substance is created in a moment's time as the words are spoken.

———— ✍ ————

Hold fast to the confession of the Word.

———— ✍ ————

This shouldn't be as strange to us as it seems, for it was by His words that God created the world. It is by His Word that we are recreated in Christ Jesus. So we are, ourselves, Word products; the products of God's own wonderful, omnipotent Word. Now, when we speak His words, we are simply acting on the authority God has given us.

Whosoever shall say unto this mountain, Be thou removed, and be thou cast into the sea; and shall not doubt in his heart, but shall believe that those things which he saith shall come to pass; he shall have whatsoever he saith.
(Mark 11:23)

We have been instructed in God's Word to *"hold fast the profession of our faith without wavering; (for he is faithful that promised)"* (Hebrews 10:23).

As we hold fast to the confession of the Word, we are to *"affirm constantly"* (Titus 3:8) those things that God has revealed to us.

But what is confession? Is it merely when we admit to wrongdoing in our lives? In the Bible, one meaning of the word *confession* means to say or affirm what God has said in His Word about a certain thing. It is agreeing with God. It is saying the same thing the Scriptures say. To hold fast our confession is to say what God has said over and over again until the thing desired in our heart and promised in the Word is fully manifested. There is no such thing as possession without confession.

When we discover the rights we have in Christ, given throughout the Bible, we are to affirm them constantly, testify to them, witness to these tremendous Bible facts. The apostle Paul said,

The communication of thy faith [will] *become effectual by the acknowledging of every good thing which is in you in Christ Jesus.* (Philemon 1:6)

Therefore, our faith will be effective only as we confess with our mouths all the good things that are ours because we belong to Jesus.

In the book of Psalms, it says, *"Let the redeemed of the LORD say so,"* (Psalm 107:2), and again, *"Let such as love thy salvation say continually, Let God be magnified"* (Psalm 70:4).

We know that in Jesus Christ we have been given salvation, not just for our souls, but for our bodies—in our health, our finances, our peace of mind, and our freedom from bondage and fear. There are hundreds of powerful affirmations to make constantly as we speak the language of the Scripture. For example:

God is who He says He is.

I am who God says I am.

God can do what He says He can do.

I can do what God says I can do.

God has what He says He has.

I have what God says I have.

———— ∽ ————

Affirmations should ring from our lips constantly.

———— ∽ ————

Affirmations of these truths should ring from our lips constantly. We are told to hold fast to them without wavering. The penalty for wavering in our confession is that we deny ourselves God's promises and the performance of them.

But let him ask in faith, nothing wavering. For he that wavereth is like a wave of the sea driven with the wind and tossed. For let not that man think that he shall receive any thing of the Lord.
(James 1:6–7)

Christianity is called the Great Confession. All things in Christ—salvation, healing, and deliverance—are dependent upon our confessing the lordship of Jesus with our lips. Paul said to Timothy, *"Thou...hast professed a good profession before many witnesses"* (1 Timothy 6:12).

"Gosh, Sir, Isn't God Wonderful?"

| DEG |

Johnny Lake was a fifteen-year-old devout Christian who lived in a town in the northern part of British Columbia. Not far from Johnny lived Dr. Riley, who had immigrated to Canada from Ireland. He was an atheist and had suffered from a painful rheumatic hip for years, but he was known throughout the area as a good doctor.

Dr. Riley took a liking to young Johnny Lake. He often took Johnny with him on house calls. One night, they were at the home of the Owens family because seven-year-old Cathy Owens was stricken with double pneumonia. As Dr. Riley listened to the girl gasping for every breath, he finally closed his black bag.

Turning to Cathy's parents, Dr. Riley sadly announced, "I'm sorry, but Cathy won't make it through the night. I must leave now to make other calls, but I'll return later. Meanwhile, I'm leaving Johnny here to sit beside Cathy."

After Dr. Riley left the house, Johnny got down on his knees so he could speak softly into Cathy's ear, "God loves you, Cathy, and God is going to heal you." Johnny whispered, "Breathe, Cathy, breathe; O God, help Cathy to breathe."

Johnny continued, "Cathy, soon it will be spring. We'll go out on the lawn; we'll make buttercups and daisy wheels. Breathe, Cathy, breathe; O God, help Cathy to breathe.

"Then, Cathy, we'll look down a gopher hole, and maybe we'll see a gopher fairy. Breathe, Cathy, breathe; O God, help Cathy to breathe!

"Then, Cathy, we'll go to the bridge and watch the minnows in the river below as the wagons go rolling across the bridge. Breathe, Cathy, breathe! Thank You, God, You are helping Cathy to breathe!"

About two hours passed before Dr. Riley returned to the Owens' home. By this time, Johnny wasn't speaking in a whisper, but with vigor and excitement. "How long has this been going on?" Dr. Riley asked Cathy's parents.

"Ever since you left, Doctor," they replied. "There were times we thought Cathy was drawing her last breath, but now it seems she is getting stronger."

Dr. Riley took out his stethoscope, bent down, and examined Cathy. He didn't say a word, but a slow smile spread across his face. Johnny jumped up and exclaimed, "God has healed Cathy! Gosh, sir, isn't God wonderful!"

Dr. Riley responded slowly as he raised himself to his full height. Placing his hand on his own afflicted hip, he spoke the name of the One he had hated for so long, "Yes, Johnny, God is wonderful!"

At that very moment, the severe pain departed from Dr. Riley's hip.

Cathy Owens was miraculously healed of double pneumonia, Dr. Riley was totally healed of his rheumatic hip, and, best of all, Dr. Riley became a deep believer in the living Christ as his Savior and Lord—all because of the power of words spoken in faith.

Proverbs 18:21 says, *"Death and life are in the power of the tongue." The Message* translation renders it like this: *"Words kill and words give life; they're either poison or fruit—you choose."*

Johnny Lake spoke words of life and faith, words of healing and blessing. When Dr. Riley broke a lifetime of rebellion by praising God, he, too, spoke words of healing—healing for his rheumatic hip. His acknowledgment of Jesus as Lord of his life brought salvation to him.

Choose to agree with God by speaking His Word.

Say it right now, "Death and life are in the power of my tongue."

God declares, "How *can two walk together except they be agreed?*" (Amos 3:3).

Your words are either life-producing or death-dealing, because when you choose to agree with God by speaking His Word, He walks with you in every area of your life.

Jesus is Lord of our affirmations. He is the Author and Finisher of our faith. He is the High Priest of our confession.

Part II

The Power in Your Words

Putting Your Best into Words

| EWK |

E mpty words hold no more interest than last year's bird nest. When we fill our words with ourselves and we are honest, our words will be honest. Others grow to depend on them.

I know a young man whose words are filled with love and unselfishness and a desire to help people. Whenever he speaks in the company of people, they listen to him.

Nowhere [else] do words have [as dramatic an effect] as they do in a radio message. The minister who speaks over the air in a cold, dead voice will get a cold, dead response. No matter how beautiful the thoughts he has or how beautifully he clothes them, if the words are not filled with love, with faith, they don't live.

Faith is built by words. Deeds have their place, but deeds are the children of words, in a large measure.

You speak, then I watch you perform. It is your speech that attracts my attention.

Your deeds have their place, and we give you credit for them, but it is your words that set us on fire.

You can fill your words with anything you wish. You can fill them with fear until the very air around you vibrates with doubt and restlessness.

You can fill your words with fear germs and you [infect] me with fear of disease and disaster. Your words [can be] filled with interrogation points, with a sense of lack, with hunger and want.

Or you come to me and your words are filled with faith. Your faith words stir me to the very depths. I wonder why I ever doubted.

Your words enwrap me within themselves. Your words are like sunlight, like coming into a warm room from a cold, frosty atmosphere outside. Your words pick up my drooping, broken spirit and fill

E. W. Kenyon

it with confidence...to go out and fight again. They are faith words, wonderful words.

The reason Jesus' words had such far-reaching influence was that they were faith words. When He said to the sea, *"Peace, be still"* [Mark 4:39], the very sea grew quiet, and the winds hushed their noise to hear the words of faith from the lips of the Man.

The deaf could hear His faith words. The lame and broken could rise and walk and run because of His faith words. There was something in His words that drove disease and pain out of the body and fear out of the heart.

Jesus' words were faith words.

I can hear [the disciple] John say, "I used exactly the same words and that boy was not healed. Now the Master takes the words out of my lips and fills them with something, and when they are heard, the child is healed."

What did Jesus put into His words that had such healing power?

A salesman is talking. He says, "I cannot understand it. I used the same argument, the same method, and I utterly failed. I used almost...identical words and yet [he] said, 'No, I cannot buy today. I have no special interest in this thing.'

"Then the other man came and took my seat. He used the same formula that I had. [The customer] became interested immediately. After awhile he reached into his pocket and pulled out his checkbook. What did that [sales]man have that I didn't?"

One man's words were filled with pure mentality. He said things like a phonograph. The other put living faith, interest, and love into his words. When this last salesman sat down, there was a look of quiet assurance on his face, and his first sentence registered because he believed in the thing he was selling.

He not only believed in it, but he believed that if the customer purchased it, it would be a blessing to him [the customer]. [He truly believed that] it was a safe and wise investment. This man generated faith, created faith in the customer.

The customer put his hand in his pocket and held it there quite a while. He was holding on to his checkbook. By and by, he said, "I will take so many shares. That looks good to me."

His check was written and signed. The deal was made. Why? Because the salesman had filled his words with faith.

The text from *Putting Your Best into Words* is taken from *Signposts on the Road to Success* by E. W. Kenyon (Kenyon's Gospel Publishing Society, 1999), 59–61.

Ordering Our Conversations Aright

|DEG|

If only we would realize the power in our words, how different our lives would be. It has been said, "The pen is mightier than the sword." How much mightier the words of our pen and of our mouth when our words are the Word of God!

God declares,

Whoso offereth praise glorifieth me: and to him that ordereth his conversation aright will I show the salvation of God. (Psalm 50:23)

Let us consider the words we use in our conversation—and let us choose wonder-working words.

Words of Confession of God's Word

Confession always precedes possession. Dare to say exactly what God says in His Word. Agree with God by speaking His Word in all circumstances.

---∽---

You provide the hands; Jesus provides the healing.

---∽---

When we order our words aright, God manifests the benefits of His great salvation. *"With the mouth confession is made unto salvation"* (Romans 10:10).

Remember that when we make confession unto salvation this includes healing, deliverance, and every spiritual and physical blessing provided for us in Christ's atonement.

Words of Praise

"I will bless the Lord at all times: his praise shall continually be in my mouth" (Psalm 34:1). Resolve to be a bold "praiser." As a praiser, extol the Lord—not so much for His gifts that you have received, but to magnify the wonderful Giver for who He is.

Words of Edification and Grace

Resolve to order your conversation aright:

Let no corrupt communication proceed out of your mouth, but that which is good to the use of edifying, that it may minister grace unto the hearers.
(Ephesians 4:29)

Words of Health

Words have great impact on our health. People enslaved by illness have a tendency to say, "I'm getting a cold," or, "I'm coming down with the flu," or, "I'm not feeling well today."

On the other hand, people who walk in divine health proclaim, "I am rarely ill because germs can't reach me," and, "I refuse to give in to illness."

Faith-Filled Words

The time to speak in faith is when you are experiencing good health and feeling great. Don't wait until you are sick to begin speaking words of health and vitality over your body. Here are words to speak daily:

Thank You, Lord Jesus, because You are my Healer. Every organ, muscle, and fiber of my body functions as You intended it to. My youth is renewed like the eagle's. My life is redeemed from destruction. I have energy to accomplish what the You have called me to do.

Words of Bold Authority Overcome Satan's Power

And they overcame him by the blood of the Lamb, and by the word of their testimony.
(Revelation 12:11)

Jesus commanded, *"Lay hands on the sick, and they shall recover"* (Mark 16:18).

You provide the hands; the Lord Jesus provides the healing! Emphasize His sure promises for *"they are life unto those that find them, and health to all their flesh"* (Proverbs 4:22).

Don't Shrink Back from Being Used by God

|DEG|

In 1979, the Lord of the harvest sent me to India. This was the beginning of a continual ministry that has resulted in hundreds of thousands of dear people receiving Christ as their personal Savior and confessing Him as Lord of their lives. The key to this ministry of the miraculous is the power of spoken faith.

Dr. Kenyon's anointed writings motivated me to list twelve affirmations on the flyleaf of my Bible. Before each service, attended by multitudes, I confess and believe these truths. If you have a genuine hunger to be used by the Lord in effective ministry, make these dynamic affirmations yours. Speak them with confidence and be enormously blessed!

∽ As I use the name of Jesus according to the Word, in the power of the Spirit, I have the secret that the apostles used to shake the world. Jesus said, "You do the asking, and I will do the doing." (See John 14:14.) If I don't pray or command in His name, I don't give Him the opportunity to manifest His power. His name on my lips is the same as if Jesus were present and operating.

∽ If I shrink back, God has no pleasure in me. (See Hebrews 10:38.) This truth has spurred me over many rough places. God can act through me. God has put His power in my hands and says, "Use My name, My Word, and My power—according to My will."

∽ I may think that the need is too great, that the sickness is unconquerable, and that my faith is too small—and all this may be true. But I have confidence in the name of Jesus, not in my own faith. In that great name, I command the sickness to go. I say, "In the name of Jesus, I command you to go." Satan dares not face a warrior who is clothed in Christ's righteousness and who knows the power of that mighty name. God's integrity, His omnipotence, and Christ's unlimited power back up my command, and are all at my disposal.

ᔿ I use the name of Jesus, though I may tremble when I do it. It is not I that am great, but that His name is great. I do not need to feel its power—I know it. Everything must bow to the all-conquering name of Jesus. What the rod was in the hands of Moses, Christ's name is in my mouth. It was not Moses who was great, but the power of God in the rod that was great.

ᔿ The only question is, "Do I understand what God means in giving me the use of His name?" To use Jesus' name does not require any unusual faith, because His name belongs to me. He has put absolutely no limitations upon the use of it. *"And whatsoever ye do in word or deed, do all in the name of the Lord Jesus, giving thanks to God and the Father by him"* (Colossians 3:17).

ᔿ I hurl the matchless name of Jesus against the hosts of hell, and they fly in confusion. I walk among men as a man of God. The enemy may be stubborn and resist me, but my will is set. I am going to win, and I literally charge the enemy in that all-conquering name. I refuse to give up my confession—that the name of Jesus is superior to all other names or things. *"God...hath highly exalted him, and given him a name which is above every name...of things in heaven, and things in earth and things under the earth"* (Philippians 2:9–10). In this great name I command the mountain to go. It will go. It must go!

⌁ God has given me the coin of the unseen kingdom. I use His name with a fearless abandonment that is absolutely thrilling. I live and walk in the realm of the supernatural. "That name has lost none of the power of the Man who bore it."[1] The Father conferred upon Him the highest name in the universe.

⌁ As I cast out devils in His name, I am amazed at the strange reverence that comes over me as I exercise—by a simple command—this marvelous power, witnessing many startling results. I cannot conceive how successful work can be done today, or how I could be in a place of continual victory over the spirits of darkness, without the name of Jesus of Nazareth, the Son of God.

⌁ "The more quickly [I] recognize that the very air about us is filled with hostile forces, who are attempting to destroy our fellowship with the Father, and to deprive us of our usefulness in the service of the Master, the better it will be for [me]."[2] All power is in the name of the risen Christ Jesus who is seated at the Father's right hand in the heavens.

᧪ I cannot effectively use the name of Jesus while out of fellowship with God. It is vitally important that I stay in fullest fellowship at every moment. If I lose my spiritual initiative, I lose something that will drive me through the hard places.

᧪ I cannot afford to take a negative attitude toward the Word. If I do, my holy fearlessness will be lost, and my heart will not say, *"I can do all things through Christ which strengtheneth me"* (Philippians 4:13). And when my spiritual initiative is low, I will not say, "Greater is He that is in me than the forces that surround me." (See 1 John 4:4.) If my heart loses its boldness and fearlessness in acting on the Word, I will be in danger.

᧪ I will take my permanent place and abide where I may enjoy the fullness of His mighty power. My confession must absolutely agree with the Word. When I have prayed or commanded in Jesus' name, I hold fast to my confession. It is easy to destroy the effect of my prayer by a negative confession. I will continue to confess that when I speak the name of Jesus it is the same as if Jesus were speaking.

Such as I have give I thee: In the name of Jesus Christ of Nazareth rise up and walk.

(Acts 3:6)

---

[1] Kenyon, E. W. *The Wonderful Name of Jesus.* (Kenyon's Gospel Publishing Society, 1998), 11.

[2] Ibid., 19

Loose Talking

| EWK |

Careless speaking is a vicious habit. When one realizes that his words are the coin of his kingdom and that his words can be [either] a cursing influence or a blessing, he will learn to value the gift of speech.

Control your tongue or it will control you. You will often hear men say, "I speak my mind." That is well if you have a good mind, but if your mind is poisoned, it is not good. An idle word spoken may fall into the soil of someone's heart and poison his whole life.

What a blessing good conversation is and what a curse its opposite!

Make your tongue a blessing, never a curse. A person is judged by his speech. Your words make you [either] a blessing or a curse. Your words may carry a fortune in them. Learn to be master of your conversation.

The text from *Loose Talking* is taken from *Signposts on the Road to Success* by E. W. Kenyon (Kenyon's Gospel Publishing Society, 1999), 32.

"Don't Break Me with Words!"

| EWK |

Don't break me with words!" This was Job's cry to his friends. (See Job 19:2.) They came as comforters. They stayed as tormentors.

Words heal and words break; words destroy and words make life as we find it today. Words heal us and words make us ill. Words bless us and words curse us. The words I just heard will linger through the day.

How little [a] woman realize[s] that a biting, stinging word in the morning will rob her husband of efficiency through a whole day. A loving, tender, beautiful word—a little prayer word—will fill him with music that will lead him on to victory. We need the...music of faith that only our loved ones can give to us.

How little we have appreciated the tremendous power of words—written words, spoken words, words set to music.

A Southern officer [after the Civil War] said to a Northern friend, "Had we had your songs, we would have conquered you."

A political speaker said, "You won the election because you had better speakers than we. We had more money, but we did not have words well spoken."

―――― ᔆ ――――

Words bless us and words curse us.

―――― ᔆ ――――

You see, men and women, a study in words is one of the most valuable assets in life. Learn how to make words work for you. Learn how to make words burn. Learn to fill words with power that cannot be resisted.

[During World War II,] Mussolini held Italy in his hand by the power of his words. Austria was conquered by Hitler with words—no powder, no poison gas, and no bayonets—just words.

How we wait for a message made up of words. The secret of advancement in life lies in the ability to say the right kind of words. My ministry over the [radio] is a ministry of words. I fill them with love; I [ask] God to fill them with Himself, and so I send them out to bless and cheer.

Mothers, your home atmosphere is a product of words. Your boy failed because wrong words were spoken; right words were not spoken.

Why is it that some children grow up so clean and strong, fight their way through college, and go out in life's fight and win? It is because the right kind of words were spoken in the home. Words make a boy love education. Words bring a boy to church or keep him away.

Think of something of infinite importance and then learn to choose the right words to express it. Then send the words out with pen or tongue. The way [you] say it has tremendous weight.

Every public speaker should make a study of words, the kind of words that count. Then, before he leaves his study, he should so charge his mind with God and God's ability that when he stands before the people, that ability will fill his words until the people are thrilled.

He should make the delivery of words a study, an art. He should fill all his words with kindness, with love....

Try out words in your own home. See how they work. Fill your lips with lovely words, beautiful words, until men will love to meet you [and] long to hear you speak. Remember, words are apples of gold in a network of silver. [See Proverbs 25:11]

The text from *"Don't Break Me with Words!"* is taken from *Signposts on the Road to Success* by E. W. Kenyon (Kenyon's Gospel Publishing Society, 1999), 64–66.

Words Can Work Blunders

|DEG|

Words can work wonders, but they can also work blunders! Do you realize that multitudes of people fail in life because they speak failure? They fear failure and allow their fear to overcome their faith.

What you say locates you. You will not—you cannot—rise above your own words. If you speak defeat, failure, anxiety, sickness, and unbelief, you will live on that level. Neither you, nor anyone else, no matter how clever, will ever live above the standard of their conversation. This spiritual principle is unalterable.

If your conversation is foolish, trifling, impractical, or disorganized, your life invariably will be the same way. With your words, you constantly paint a public picture of your inner self. Jesus said, *"Out of the abundance of the heart the mouth speaketh"* (Matthew 12:34).

If you think back on your life, you will probably agree that most of your troubles have been tongue troubles. The Bible says, *"Whoso keepeth his mouth and his tongue keepeth his soul from troubles"* (Proverbs 21:23).

Oh, the trouble caused by an unruly tongue! Words spoken in the heat of the moment—words of anger, words of harshness, words of retaliation, words of bitterness, words of unkindness—these words produce trouble for us. Beloved, let's make this our prayer right now:

Let the words of my mouth, and the meditation of my heart, be acceptable in thy sight, O LORD, my strength, and my redeemer. (Psalm 19:14)

Here's another good Bible prayer: *"Set a watch, O LORD, before my mouth; keep the door of my lips"* (Psalm 141:3).

It's really important that we let God help us overcome our unruly speech habits, for our words can work blunders and get us into trouble. A negative confession can produce negative results. The Bible warns, *"Thou art snared with the words of thy*

mouth, thou art taken with the words of thy mouth"
(Proverbs 6:2).

Confession is made with the mouth, not only
for the good things God has promised us, but
also for sickness, defeat, bondage, lack, and failure.

Refuse to have a bad confession. Refuse to
have a negative confession. Repudiate a dual confession when you are saying at one moment, *"with
his stripes we are healed"* (Isaiah 53:5), and at the
next moment, "But the pain is still there."

Most of our troubles are tongue troubles.

Go to higher level of living in the kingdom
of God. Believe you are who God says you are.
Think that way. Talk that way. Act that way.
Train yourself to live on the level of what is written in God's Word about you.

Do not permit your thoughts, your words, or
your actions to contradict what God says about
you.

Although you may not master positive confession in a day, or even a week, you will learn it as
you continue to walk in it faithfully. Because He
has said it, we may boldly say the same thing!

Just a Word of Warning

| EWK |

Children's lives are largely made up of words—the words of their parents and those whom they love and admire. A mother can fill her boy's heart with zeal for an education and for a position in life, or she can, with words, destroy the finest spirit that was ever given to a home....

[A] wife little appreciates the power of [her] words on her husband's life. [If] he loses his job, she could scold him and tell him that he is no good. He was whipped before he came home, but he would then be doubly whipped.

Instead, she puts her arms around him and says, "That's all right, dear. You will get a better position. You are worthy of a better job anyway."

He goes out the next morning thrilled by the touch of her lips....[Her] words have filled him with courage and confidence. He leaves her heart filled with joy and gladness, and she says, "What a man God gave me." He says, "What a woman you gave me, Lord." They have learned the secret of words.

A few devastating words could have filled his mind with confusion, his heart with pain, and his eyes with tears. Words give heartache, [or] words give strength and comfort and faith.

Let's be careful of the words we use. Don't tell that story you heard the other day about this man or that woman. Don't let any other ears be poisoned as your ears have been poisoned with it.

Never repeat scandal. Never repeat the calamity things. Let others do the talking about that. You keep your lips for beautiful things, helpful things, comforting things. That is your job.

The text from *Just a Word of Warning* is taken from *Signposts on the Road to Success* by E. W. Kenyon (Kenyon's Gospel Publishing Society, 1999), 38–39.

Wailing and Failing Go Hand in Hand

|DEG|

Whoso keepeth his mouth and his tongue keepeth his soul from troubles.
—Proverbs 21:23

Thou art snared with the words of thy mouth, thou art taken [captive] with the words of thy mouth.
—Proverbs 6:2

Jesus promised us a saved, healed life; a Spirit-filled life. Here in this Scripture from Proverbs 21, He promises to rescue our soul from every trouble—*"all things work together for good to them that love God"* (Romans 8:28)—if we "keep" our mouths and our tongues.

Thousands of Christians wonder, "Why is my life seemingly loaded with trouble and heartache? Why does my life have more bad than good? Why am I defeated, sick, and miserable so much of the time? Why am I beaten down and feeling hopeless?"

You may wonder, "I'm a believer. But why the misery? Why am I unhappy?"

The answer is that, with your own words, you have opened the door to Satan. When you speak death-dealing words, you give Satan permission to come into your life, into your affairs.

Just what are wrong words? Which words give Satan access to your life? Here are some classic examples:

"I'll always be in debt."

"I think I'm coming down with something."

"It looks like we won't be able to pay our bills this month."

"Satan is on me all the time. I just can't defeat him."

"Well, if it's bad, it will happen to me."

"I just know we'll have an accident."

"I guess we will have to give up the idea of ever having a home of our own."

"It seems like bad things always happen to us."

"I am afraid I'm stuck in this situation."

"We'll just have to put up with this."

"These kids will never make it at the rate they are going."

"I guess we won't get a vacation this year."

—— ∽ ——
Speak in faith, not in fear.
—— ∽ ——

"My folks always had poor health, so I probably will, too."

"My marriage doesn't look like it's going to make it."

"I just don't love my husband/wife any-more."

"The children don't love me. They won't obey me."

"It just seems we will never get anywhere."

"This family is going to the dogs."

"My family just doesn't want God."

When Jesus said in Mark 11:23, "[You] *shall have whatsoever* [you] *saith,*" He was describing a powerful law of faith that works for good or bad, for sickness or health, for supply or lack, for defeat or victory. When you speak words like the ones listed above, you give place to Satan.

Satan will deliver to you what you have said. He seems to say, in his destructive way, "You've declared these things, and you can trust me to do them. I surely won't fail you."

Unless you speak in faith, your enemy will see to it that you reach the level of your own words.

Be Humble or You Will Tumble

|DEG|

F aith is a fruit of humility. *"God resisteth the proud, but giveth grace unto the humble"* (James 4:6). One of the most challenging yet triumphant experiences of my life involved the relationship between true humility and the confession of God's Word for healing.

In 1976, I was oppressed with very painful headaches from the top of my head to the back of my neck. The pain was nearly more than I could stand. I had received miraculous healings from both an enlarged heart and a cancerous growth as a result of boldly speaking God's Word, but though I spoke the healing Word repeatedly, my headaches were unrelenting. Finally, I visited my family physician. He assured me that he could give me a prescription that would take care of the headaches. He was sincerely mistaken.

Weeks dragged by, and the headaches remained my primary concern. Then we went overseas for ministry.

———— ∽ ————
Faith is a fruit of humility.
———— ∽ ————

I was going through the daily speaking assignments, ministering mostly by rote. With the intense pain in my head, I could hardly concentrate on anything else. One day, a high school principal and his wife made my wife and me their special guests for a tour of the area and a nice lunch. However, the pain was increasing to such a level that I could barely endure the day's activities.

After preaching that night, depression and self-pity hit me like a blast of dynamite. I tumbled into bed with these morbid words: "I don't want to live another day. I hope I will die in my sleep tonight. These pains are so miserable, I just can't stand them." My wife was not impressed by my negativity.

After a fitful night, I awakened to discover my prayer was not answered: I was still alive. I announced to my wife that I was going to the prayer closet in our friend's home, and I wasn't going to come out until I heard from the Lord about my wretched condition. When I arrived at the prayer closet, I locked the door from the inside so no one could disturb me.

The words of Psalm 34:6 came forcibly to me, *"This poor man cried, and the LORD heard him, and saved him out of all his troubles."*

I felt as if I was that desperate man as I stretched myself out on the carpet of that room. I cried out with tears, "Lord, why has my healing not been manifested? I have confessed Your healing Word, I have praised Your name, and I have searched my heart. I have prayed and fasted. Why have I not received my healing?"

The Holy Spirit responded to my request for Him to search my heart and reveal the hindrance to my healing. He made known to me that I had a spirit of pride that was preventing the manifestation of healing for my excruciating headaches.

Quickly the Scriptures began to rise up in my spirit:

Be clothed with humility: for God resisteth the proud, and giveth grace to the humble. Humble yourselves therefore under the mighty hand of God, that He may exalt you in due time.

(1 Peter 5:5–6)

[Serve] *the Lord with all humility.*
(Acts 20:19)

He hath showed thee, O man, what is good; and
what doth the Lord require of thee, but to do
justly, and to love mercy, and to walk humbly
with thy God? (Micah 6:8)

The Holy Spirit spoke these words to my spirit: "Any time you are proud, the Lord must resist you. If your prayers are not answered, if your finances are not being provided, if you are not receiving your healing, you must examine your heart to see if you are permitting pride to prevent your request."

A High Price For Low Living

Now, if you had asked me if I thought I was bound by an attitude of pride, I would have said, "No."

The Lord showed me that it was not so much an attitude of arrogance or egotism I had. Rather, it was an attitude of self-sufficiency. My spirit was not one of dependence on Him.

When I realized that this attitude of pride was keeping God from healing me of the headaches, I cried out, "Lord, what a high price for low living! Forgive me, Lord, for having such a wrong spirit. Never again do I want to possess this attitude of pride. Cleanse me, Lord, by your precious blood."

God forgave me and cleansed me from that ugly spirit of pride.

We need to have an attitude of dependence on God.

For the next forty-five minutes, I basked in His presence; praising the Lord and confessing His healing Word.

As I continued to speak the Word, I looked up and saw a man standing in the room. I quickly looked to see if the door was still locked. It was.

The stranger moved slowly toward me as I lay on the floor. He reached down and laid his hand on my head. The sensation of his touch was like warm, penetrating oil flowing into my head. All of the pain instantly left! The man stepped back, keeping his gaze on me.

I wanted this stranger to identify himself, so I asked him, "Sir, are you the apostle Paul?" I have no explanation for why I asked that question. I just knew I was a part of something tremendously supernatural.

The man replied, "I am an angel of the Lord sent to minister to you who are an heir of salvation." (That is exactly what Hebrews 1:14 declares.) After he spoke those words, the angel vanished from my sight. I never saw him again.

I sat there simply amazed that an angel of the Lord had visited me. I was healed, praise God! That day, a new "Power Poem" was born into my spirit: "Be humble or you will tumble!"

Indeed, faith is a fruit of true humility. My confession of the healing Scriptures did not minister healing until I humbled my heart and dealt with my attitude of pride.

The story I've just told you occurred in February 1976. More than twenty-five years have passed since that wonderful miracle, and it is still one of the sweetest supernatural happenings of my entire life.

Equally important is this awesome fact: I have never had a headache since that long-ago day on a faraway island!

Yes, there was a satanic trap set for me the day I arrived back home, but I resisted the lying vanities that the enemy tried to push on me. Boldly I declared, "Listen, Devil, I was healed by the bleeding stripes of Jesus my Lord. You are a wicked thief who is trying to steal my healing. I refuse to be your dumping ground any longer. Be gone, Devil, in the mighty name of Jesus!"

I don't expect to have a headache ever again. Jesus dispatched His holy angel to minister that deliverance for me.

Oh, for a thousand tongues to sing my dear Savior's praise for this mighty deliverance!

"Did You Really See an Angel?"

One Sunday morning, when I was in Cairns, Queensland, Australia, ministering at an Assemblies of God church, I shared this account of the visitation of the angel of the Lord and the wondrous healing I received.

After the service, a lady named Mrs. Clarke approached me with her fifteen-year-old daughter, Cathy. "Mr. Gossett," the mother said, "my daughter has a question she wants to ask you."

I turned to the daughter. She asked, "Did you really see an angel?"

"Yes, I did, Cathy."

She gazed at me a few moments then added, "Really?" Again, I assured her that what I had shared about the visit of the angel was completely true.

Then I spoke to her, "Cathy, I have a question I would like to ask, a question far more important than the one you asked me. Have you received Jesus Christ as your personal Savior and Lord?"

She replied, "No, I haven't."

"Then, Cathy, I want to ask you another question: Would you like to accept the Lord today, right here and now?"

Without a moment's hesitation, Cathy answered, "Yes, Mr. Gossett, I would like to do that right now." I had the joy of leading her to Jesus that Sunday morning.

She was fascinated by my testimony of being visited by an angel. My answers to her questions satisfied her. Most important, she walked away from that church a born-again child of God. That really is the most important matter!

Part III

The Fruits of Spoken Faith

We Have Victory in Jesus' Name

| EWK |

The night which caused me to write the song, "We Have Victory in Jesus' Name," was a fearful night. All day it had stormed. The wind whipped up into a fury, and the snow had piled up in great drifts. It stormed as only it can storm on that fearful eastern coast [of the United States].

The crowd had come. Conviction was so great that it seemed like nothing could keep the folks away. Drifts were high. They had to wade through the snow to get there.

Oh, how the wind shrieked and howled that night. A voice could scarcely be heard above the noise of the elements. It seemed like the fury of hell was let loose around us.

I turned to a young man who travelled with me, and who was mighty in prayer, and said, "Theodore, will you pray?"

He got up and tried to pray, but the wind drowned out his voice, and in a moment he broke down and gave up.

Then I turned to his wife, who was also mighty in prayer, and asked her to lead, and she broke, too. All the demons of hell seemed to be let loose on us....

—— ∽ ——

The audience was hushed in the presence and power of Jesus' name.

—— ∽ ——

I was walking the platform [as] Nellie was trying to pray, and when she gave up, I stepped forward and charged the elements in the name of Jesus to cease. I rebuked the storm.

In a moment, it became calm. It wasn't the dying down of the wind. It wasn't the gradual subsiding. It had seemed I couldn't raise my voice above the tumult, and when the storm ceased, before I finished praying, I found that I was actually yelling.

I became quiet. The audience became hushed and awed in the presence and power of that name. It was in the name of Jesus.

———— ✍ ————

The text from *We Have Victory in Jesus' Name* is taken from "The Miracle of the Book of John" (unpublished sermon), preached June 1928, 15–16, as quoted in *E. W. Kenyon and His Message of Faith: The True Story* by Joe McIntyre (Lake Mary, FL: Charisma House, 1997), 268–269.

———— ✍ ————

Boldy Say What God Says

|DEG|

For he hath said, I will never leave thee, nor forsake thee. So that we may boldly say, The Lord is my helper, and I will not fear what man shall do unto me.
—Hebrews 13:5–6

Make God's Word the standard for your life. Train yourself to say what He says. Bring your lips under subjection. Think before you speak. Say what God says! Don't contradict Him and His Word. God is in His Word. When you confess it, He performs it! Sooner than you can imagine, a revolution will take place in your life.

When you do these things, you will find that you are truly living the bold, abundant life set forth in God's Word. I know this for certain because it has happened innumerable times in my own life and ministry.

I am blessed over and over as I remember how God provided for us in our first mission to Africa years ago. We were down to the last day before leaving that February, but we were still seventeen hundred dollars short of the necessary funds for the mission.

———— ✍ ————
Walk with God by agreeing with God.
———— ✍ ————

No matter what avenue I had pursued in obtaining the money, none had been successful. But I knew this was a time to hold my heart steady in the expectation that God Himself would minister to our need.

I quietly reaffirmed again and again, both in my heart and with my mouth, what the word promised: *"My God shall supply all your need according to his riches in glory by Christ Jesus"* (Philippians 4:19).

Arriving at my office that last morning, I called all our staff together. We decided we would walk with God by agreeing with God—just as I had boldly preached to thousands of others to do.

We presented our need for seventeen hundred dollars to our heavenly Father. Then we lifted up our hands and praised the Lord in advance for His supply. We confessed the Word together for a time before returning to the normal duties of the day. We were not trying to manipulate God, nor even to "impress Him" with our earnestness in seeking His help. We were simply requesting provision from our faithful God.

While I was gone from the office, a man from Vancouver named Peter Dyck called and told my wife, "The Lord has spoken to me by His sweet inner voice, 'Give Don Gossett seventeen hundred dollars.' I don't have that much money in my bank account, but I made a loan on my credit card to secure the cash. If Brother Don can meet me on my way to work this afternoon, I will have the seventeen hundred dollars to give him."

This was one of the most miraculous divine interventions we had experienced up to that time. The Lord spoke the exact amount we needed, and the man heard His voice and obeyed Him!

I never cease to marvel at those dear people who can hear the voice of the Lord and obey Him. During a meeting that I held at a Baptist church in Duanesberg, New York, a man named Sam Sumner stood and shared this testimony:

After I was baptized in the Holy Spirit several years ago, I was walking in a wondrous time of Spirit-led events that were beautiful. Then one day the Lord said to me, "I want you to send Don Gossett three hundred dollars."

I replied, "All right, Lord, I will. But I don't know who Don Gossett is, where he lives, or just how I could send him three hundred dollars."

I more or less forgot about that word until a few weeks passed. Then the Lord spoke rather firmly, "When are you going to send Don Gossett the three hundred dollars I told you to send him?"

I was a little upset about this reminder. After all, I didn't even know who Don Gossett was, or how to send him the money. I walked out to my car complaining, "Lord, you have got to let me know how I can do this!"

I drove out on the New York Thruway and turned on the radio. I was just surfing the dial when I heard these words: "You can write to Don Gossett, Box 2, Blaine, Washington, 98231." Praise God, it was like a voice from heaven!

It is quite remarkable how the Lord can speak with His inner voice and how the hearts of sincere people can hear Him and have the grace to obey lovingly.

Through a lifetime of trusting God for many things, I have learned that God desires us to speak in faith. God's responses are normally preceded by our faith words. The Lord says, *"To him that ordereth his conversation aright will I show the salvation of God"* (Psalm 50:23).

We are not mere robots without the ability to choose the words we speak. Rather, we order our conversation rightly or wrongly. God gives guidance to our conversation and motivates our words, but the choice to order our conversation is still ours. God says, "If you choose to order your conversation aright, I will show you my salvation." By this, He means salvation in every area of our lives.

Healed by Jesus of Nazareth...in Nazareth

Several years ago, I led a group of Christians to Israel. As we left Jerusalem early one morning, I was battling an intense fever, which meant there was infection raging inside me. I felt miserable as we continued our sightseeing through Israel. It was quite a battle for me.

I knew I shouldn't talk about it with my friends. I would certainly get their sympathy and pity and begin to feel sorry for myself. None of those factors would help when what I needed was healing from God. I continued to quietly maintain my confession of His Word.

As I disciplined my heart and lips to speak, "Thank You, Jesus, by Your stripes I am healed" (see 1 Peter 2:24), the Lord was gracious to manifest a beautiful healing for me in the city of Nazareth, the hometown of our Lord Jesus Christ.

I immediately conducted a healing service right there on the streets of Nazareth. I announced to my group of thirty-five companions, "Most of last night and all day, I have battled a raging fever. I took a brief nap here on the bus. When I awoke, I was perspiring profusely. The fever has broken! Jesus of Nazareth has healed me right here in Nazareth!"

They all rejoiced with me. Then, I ministered to those who needed healing, and His power and love were manifested.

I would like to say to you reading this book that right now you can begin to speak the Word and Jesus of Nazareth will be your healer, whether you live in Canada, the United States, England, Barbados, India, or some other place. Simply hold fast to your confession, saying, "By His stripes I am healed."

"As thy days, so shall thy strength be" (Deuteronomy 33:25). It is essential that you take the Lord's strength daily. We all know our weaknesses in life—whether spiritual, physical, or mental. Sometimes our weaknesses are in our conversations, bad habits, overindulgence in eating, watching too much television, or being consumed with unclean sexual desires and thoughts.

We have victory over those weaknesses because the Lord knows how to minister strength. Let's confess His Word, *"The LORD is the strength of my life"* (Psalm 27:1), or *"Let the weak say, I am strong"* (Joel 3:10).

God gives us grace to overcome adversity.

Say it over and over: "In Jesus I am strong! I am strong!" If that seems like a contradiction to your natural thinking, consider that you are moving to a higher level of life where God's Word prevails, not your negative feelings and thoughts.

The Christian life is made up of a series of adversities and problems, which God always gives us the grace to overcome. That's why God calls us "overcomers," not "those going under."

Financial Mountains

Verily I say unto you, That whosoever shall say unto this mountain, Be thou removed, and be thou cast into the sea; and shall not doubt in his heart, but shall believe that those things which he saith shall come to pass; he shall have whatsoever he saith. (Mark 11:23)

Notice Jesus did not say, "He shall have whatsoever he thinketh." Positive thinking is powerful, but it's not "he shall have whatsoever he thinketh," rather, *"he shall have whatsoever he saith."*

Since the Holy Spirit taught me the enormous importance of "speaking to mountains," my finances have been literally transformed. I would like to share two of my more recent experiences. The first story involves God's provision through the help of a stranger.

Because my wife, Debra, and I are called to preach to the nations, we travel more than one hundred thousand miles every year. We have always spoken in faith for the money necessary to purchase our many airline fares and, in 1997, the Lord responded to our spoken faith by touching the heart of one of His choice saints. This lady has been a listener to my daily radio broadcasts for many years, and she often heard our reports of traveling to India, Africa, and other nations.

God Himself dropped into her heart a burden to provide complimentary tickets for our ministry. This lady has worked for one of the largest airlines in the world for more than twenty years. Through her connection with the airline, she was able to secure tickets called "Companion Passes," which she gave to us.

We, almost reluctantly, approached the airline counter with those passes in hand, and I simply told the agent we wanted to go to Hong Kong then on to Delhi, India. They promptly issued our boarding passes, and we were on our way. And not just in ordinary economy seating—we were assigned seats in business class! I was caught up with a sense of wonder.

I thought, "Not only do we have these expensive business class seats, but the price is so right— free! Praise the Lord!"

Since 1997, we have taken dozens of these wonderful flights. Singapore. Tokyo. Paris. Frankfurt. Delhi. Hong Kong. Milan. Sydney. Melbourne. Had we paid for these flights, the cost would have been tens of thousands of dollars.

The second story is about God's provision of a car.

Before my dear first wife, Joyce, received her call to heaven, she helped me to buy a new car. That was in April 1989. For ten years, I delighted in driving that car, adding many thousands of miles each year.

As the car slowly began to deteriorate, my children would often say to me, "Dad, it's time for you to buy a new car."

I always responded to them by simply saying, "No, since 1950 I've signed notes and gone into debt for many different vehicles. Not again! This time, I'm going to speak the Word of the Lord for the provision of new transportation."

Speak to your mountains.

Debra and I continued to speak for this provision. Then on March 17, 1999, I received a phone call from a Christian brother.

"Don, I want you and Debra to see me at my office today. Can you come?"

"Yes," I responded, "We will be there."

Upon arrival at the man's office, he invited us to go for a ride in his vehicle. After a few blocks, he asked me to drive the vehicle. Then, later, he suggested that Debra drive. When we returned to his office, he asked, "How do you like the vehicle?" We assured him it was very nice indeed.

Astonishingly, the man replied, "Since you like it, it's yours! Come back tomorrow and we'll have the paperwork done, and you can take the car."

Again, this was so completely in the realm of the supernatural that we were beside ourselves with joy and delight.

You see, this was not just an ordinary vehicle. It was a 1998 Range Rover, the top of the line in the Land Rover family. We were informed it was the official vehicle of the royal family in England—where the car is made. When we saw a video describing the unique features of this Range Rover, we were once more walking on fleecy clouds of spiritual ecstasy.

Since March 1999, Debra and I have enjoyed driving this car immensely! Again, it was the Lord's provision in response to our belief-filled spoken faith. Only God could have supernaturally directed this man to be His instrument of supply. And that man could hear the voice of the Lord and obey!

"He shall have whatsoever he saith."

Who said those words? Our Master the Lord Jesus Christ!

Did He really mean it? Yes!

Does it include finances? Most assuredly!

These two remarkable provisions have been the "icing on the cake" during our many years of speaking the Word for finances.

Need a job? Or a better job? Need a good car? Need money to roof your home? Need new furniture to replace the worn-out items in your home? Need money for dental bills? Need funds for your children's education? Need money for airline tickets?

Whether your area of need is financial, spiritual, or physical, this is my challenge to you:

- Don't talk sickness; rather speak the healing Word.

- Don't talk weakness; rather affirm that the Lord is the strength of your life.

- Don't talk defeat; rather shout your victory in Jesus.

- Don't talk lack; rather confess His provision for your every need.

- Don't talk bondage; rather confess His freedom.

Centurion's Faith

|DEG|

As Jesus entered the village of Capernaum, a Roman captain came up in a panic and said, "Master, my servant is sick. He can't walk. He's in terrible pain."

Jesus said, "I'll come and heal him."

"Oh, no," said the captain. "I don't want to put you to all that trouble. Just give the order and my servant will be fine. I'm a man who takes orders and gives orders. I tell one soldier, 'Go,' and he goes; to another, 'Come,' and he comes; to my slave, 'Do this,' and he does it."

Taken aback, Jesus said, "I've yet to come across this kind of simple trust in Israel, the very people *who are supposed to know all about God and how he works. This man is the vanguard of many outsiders who will soon be coming from all directions—streaming in from the east, pouring in from the west, sitting down at God's kingdom banquet alongside Abraham, Isaac, and Jacob.*

"Then those who grew up 'in the faith' but had no faith will find themselves out in the cold, outsiders to grace and wondering what happened."

Then Jesus turned to the captain and said, "Go. What you believed could happen has happened." At that moment his servant became well.

(Matthew 8:5–13 MESSAGE)

This is one of my favorite Bible stories. It sets forth all the divine ingredients of triumphant faith—the power of spoken faith in action.

How do you exercise the power of spoken faith? *"The word is nigh thee, even in thy mouth, and in thy heart: that is, the word of faith, which we preach"* (Romans 10:8). It is exercised by believing the Word in your heart and speaking it with your mouth. The centurion of Matthew 8 understood and practiced the power of spoken faith, and Jesus highly commended him. In fact, He called the centurion's faith the greatest faith He had seen in all Israel.

We can speak with the same spirit of faith. *"It is written, I believed, and therefore have I spoken; we also believe, and therefore speak"* (2 Corinthians 4:13).

Believe and speak. Salvation, the greatest of all God's gifts, comes to us by the believing heart and the confessing mouth. (See Romans 10:9.) When we learn to speak the Word and not the problem, we are on the road to absolute victory. But we are defeated the moment we allow ourselves to start listing our burdens instead of counting our blessings. God bestows His benefits on a daily basis. It should also be a daily matter for us to praise Him.

God bestows His benefits on a daily basis.

It would probably surprise us if we knew how much answered prayer depends on our attitude of praise to God. The key to answered requests is that prayer unlocks the door and praise keeps it open. Once we start praising Him, we can never really justify stopping because there is no end to His greatness, or to our reasons for being grateful. We all go to Him in prayer, but how many times do we return to praise Him? Remember how Jesus felt about the thankless lepers in Luke 17:

And as he entered into a certain village, there met him ten men that were lepers, which stood afar off: And they lifted up their voices, and said, Jesus, Master, have mercy on us. And when he saw them, he said unto them, Go show yourselves unto the priests. And it came to pass, that, as they went, they were cleansed. And one of them, when he saw that he was healed, turned back, and with a loud voice glorified God, and fell down on his face at his feet, giving him thanks: and he was a Samaritan. And Jesus answering said, Were there not ten cleansed? but where are the nine? There are not found that returned to give glory to God, save this stranger.

(Luke 17:12–18)

By Your Words

|EWK|

Perhaps [no one ever] told you, but [people] measure you by your words. You are rated by your words. Your salary is gauged by the value of your words. Your words make a place for you in the business in which you are engaged.

Neither jealousy nor fear can keep you from climbing to the top if your words have value that belongs at the top. The organization is bound to give you the place that belongs to you if your words bring forth the right results.

You don't have to put on; you don't have to exaggerate. All you have to do is to be natural, but make that "natural" worth listening to.

Study your work. Study how to say things. Study how to use words that will change circumstances around you. Make a study, an analytical study of words, then see how much you can put into a single sentence. I don't mean how many words, but how much you can put into the words so that when men and women listen to your words, they will be thrilled by them.

How are you going to bless others?

The clerk in a five-and-ten-cent store said, "Good morning," in such a way that I turned to look at her. She had put something into her words. She had put herself, her personality, into her words. Her words rang. She sold me some pencils at two for five cents, but sold them as though she were selling a Pierce-Arrow car. After I had left the store, I felt inclined to go back and watch her deal with other customers.

Cut out the useless words that stand in the way. Eliminate all the words that would hinder... [your words] from reaching the mark. Trust in words. Trust in the words of your own lips. Fill them with loving truth.

Think in your heart how you want to help those who are to be your customers, how you are going to bless them, and how the thing that you have is necessary to their enjoyment. It is what you put into words that makes them live in the hearts of the hearers.

Empty words die in no-man's-land. They never get over the trench. If they do, they are duds. If they do get across and people hear them, they amount to nothing. Living words—words bursting with heart messages—thrill and grip.

Love always seeks the right word to convey its message without loss [of meaning] in transit. Clothe your thoughts in the most beautiful words, but don't sacrifice pungency for beauty—blend them.

All He Had Were Words

This is a little study of great things. One man started out in life without sponsors, without a university education, without money. Someone said to him, "What have you beside your two hands to make a success in life?"

He said softly, "I have nothing but words." The friend smiled, not understanding him.

So he started on his lonely quest for success with nothing but words. He learned the secret of putting things into words, of making words living things. He [loaded] his words with thought, clear thought, and, after a bit, he learned the secret of putting his fine, clean, splendid manhood into his words.

Men began to set a value upon his words. People would stop him on the street to engage him in conversation just to hear his words.

You understand that almost every man who has climbed to the top of the ladder of success has climbed with words.

Here and there, a man has climbed because of an unusual voice or an unusual gift of artistry, but the majority of men have gotten their feet on the first rung of the ladder of success by words. They climbed, rung by rung, to the top.

Many use words to climb the ladder of success.

A man must put a valuation on his own words before others will sense their value. The ambitious man's words became his bank account. He studied, he dug deep, he thought through...problems. Other people learned to trust his judgment and his words, rather than to study for themselves.

There is a vast army of people who have certain business ability, but they have to hire others to do most of their thinking. He [the ambitious man] supplied that want. He did the thinking. By and by, they were willing to pay him almost any price to have him think for them.

His words became valuable. They were his servants. How they labored for him! He filled words with inspiration, with comfort, with hope for others.

He sent them out on wings, until they passed from house to house, from lip to lip. He found himself being quoted here and there. His words were doing things....He had learned the secret of words. By and by, publishers paid him unthinkable prices for his words. Why? Because he had learned the art of filling words with inspiration, [with] new life.

Let's study words. Let's learn to fill them with goodies for the children, healing for the sick, and victory for the discouraged, and we will win.

The text from *By Your Words* is taken from *Signposts on the Road to Success* by E. W. Kenyon (Kenyon's Gospel Publishing Society, 1999), 55–58.

Speak the Word Only

|DEG|

I want to share one of the most wonderful testimonies of healing I have ever heard. It happened in a hospital in London, England, in March, 1994. I can, perhaps, relate this story better than anyone else can, because I was deeply involved in it.

My daughter, Judy, and I were traveling in East Africa doing crusades. In Nairobi, Kenya, we had several services every day, and Judy led a hundred-voice choir every night.

Following the crusades in Nairobi, we flew to Mombassa, by the Indian Ocean, for further ministry. The heat and humidity in Mombassa make it one of the most intolerable cities in the world for living accommodations. It was terribly hot, but Judy and I worked very hard while we were there.

Then came the day we were to fly to London for an overnight stay before we returned to North America. After we were airborne, Judy told me that she was going to another part of the jet where she had seen several empty seats and could stretch out a bit more. About halfway through the ten-hour flight, I went back to talk with her and make sure she was okay.

"Dad, I've vomited several times," she informed me. I placed my hand on her forehead and prayed a brief, fatherly prayer for her, then returned to my seat. It seemed like something minor; I wasn't overly concerned.

The Crisis

About a half hour before we landed in London, a flight attendant found me and related this grave news.

"Mr. Gossett, I'm sorry to inform you that your daughter, Judy, is a very sick lady. Not only has she vomited many times, she is also hemorrhaging from every opening in her body.

"It is the blood that has us alarmed. We don't know if it's food poisoning or just what the problem is. We have notified Heathrow Airport to meet the flight with a wheelchair for your daughter."

The wheelchair was waiting when we landed, and they took Judy to a medical examining room. After more than an hour, a doctor came out with more critical news: "Mr. Gossett, we have taken blood from your daughter. She has something more severe than parasites, but beyond that we are uncertain. We have ordered an ambulance to come immediately and take her across London to a hospital that specializes in tropical and infectious diseases."

Receive His healing and provision for your life.

"Please, doctor, that won't be necessary. Judy worked very hard while we were in Africa. I'm sure she will be all right with a good night's rest, and I've booked rooms for us tonight here in London," I explained.

The doctor was quite blunt as she responded to my protest. "Mr. Gossett, leaving the hospital is not an option. Your daughter has been quarantined. She's now the responsibility of British Airways and the city of London. There is no way we would consider permitting her to leave with the highly contagious disease she may have."

At about that time, two men rolled out a stretcher with Judy strapped to it. They told me that I could accompany her to the hospital, so I rode sitting next to Judy in the ambulance. She looked so weak considering the strength she usually exudes.

She looked up at me and said, "Dad, I've never been in a hospital a day or night in my life. I wasn't even born in a hospital."

"I know all of that, Judy. But you are going to be all right; God will see you through." I tried to encourage her.

When we arrived at the hospital, a whole battery of doctors and nurses met us. They were all wearing emergency-looking hospital garments and quickly took her away to an isolation room.

After a long time, Dr. Clark, the chief physician, came out to speak to me.

"Mr. Gossett, your daughter is an extremely ill woman. We will do our best to save her life, but we won't know anything until morning. Meanwhile, you will have to leave the hospital, and you won't be permitted to return until we notify you that you can.

"You may enter the isolation room where your daughter is, but only for twenty minutes. Then you must leave the hospital."

When I was alone with Judy, I told her, "Judy, the doctor has given me only twenty minutes with you before I must leave. We won't have time for deep intercessions for you. But Judy, I'm going to speak the healing Word for you. I have these truths in my spirit—in my 'alphabet of healing.' Remember, Jesus cast out evil spirits with His Word; that's what I'm going to do now. The Word I speak over you will expel these spirits of infirmity and disease. Just receive this Word as I speak it now. Any one of these twenty-six verses can be your healing portion."

I began with the letter **A**:

Attend to my words; incline thine ear unto my sayings. Let them not depart from thine eyes; keep them in the midst of thine heart. For they are life unto those that find them, and health to all their flesh. (Proverbs 4:20–22)

I said, "Judy, His Word is health to all your flesh. This is for you right now; receive His healing provision for your life!"

Then I went on to the letter **B**: *"Beloved, I wish above all things that thou mayest prosper and be in health, even as thy soul prospereth"* (3 John 2).

"O beloved Judy, God our Father really wants you to be in health, not in this devastating sickness; it's yours to receive now."

When I spoke the letter **C**, I repeated this prayer of David: *"Create in me a clean heart, O God; and renew a right spirit within me"* (Psalm 51:10).

I said, "Judy, I believe you have a clean heart and a right spirit. Let's allow the Holy Spirit to do His work of heart-searching and renewal as we yield to Him now."

After Judy and I quietly allowed the Holy Spirit to do His blessed work of cleansing and renewal, we went to the letter **D**: *"Deal bountifully with thy servant, that I may live, and keep thy word"* (Psalm 119:17).

Knowing Judy's very life was at stake, I urgently spoke this letter **D** over her! "That she may live, Lord, and keep your Word!"

The letter **E**: *"Effectual fervent prayer of a righteous man availeth much"* (James 5:16).

The letter **F** reminded us of God's mercies through the past years. *"Forget not all his benefits: who forgiveth all thine iniquities; who healeth all thy diseases"* (Psalm 103:2–3).

I boldly spoke the letter **G**:

God anointed Jesus of Nazareth with the Holy Ghost and with power: who went about doing good, and healing all that were oppressed of the devil; for God was with him. (Acts 10:38)

When I spoke the letter **H**, I sought to impress upon Judy this eternal fact: *"He* [Jesus] *took up our infirmities and carried our diseases"* (Matthew 8:17 NIV).

I affirmed that God's original healing covenant was expressed in the letter **I**: *"I am the Lord that healeth thee"* (Exodus 15:26).

Honoring our Lord's majesty came with the letter **J**: *"Jesus Christ the same yesterday, and to day, and for ever"* (Hebrews 13:8).

The letter **K**:

> *Know ye not that your body is the temple of the Holy Ghost which is in you, which ye have of God, and ye are not your own? For ye are bought with a price: therefore glorify God in your body, and in your spirit, which are God's.*
> (1 Corinthians 6:19–20)

When I spoke the letter **L**—*"Lay hands on the sick, and they shall recover"* (Mark 16:18), I assured Judy that I would lay hands on her and that Jesus Himself promised she would recover.

M is precious: *"Merry heart doeth good like a medicine"* (Proverbs 17:22).

N magnifies the strong name above all other names:

> [Jesus'] *name through faith in his name hath made this man strong, whom ye see and know: yea,*

the faith which is by him hath given him this perfect soundness in the presence of you all.

(Acts 3:16)

The very next day, Judy was to tell me that the letter **O** proved to be the quickening Word, the very rhema of God that ministered healing to her. She declared that after I spoke this letter **O**, she never vomited again, nor did she pass any more blood! What was the dynamic letter **O**?

Ought not this woman, being a daughter of Abraham, whom Satan hath bound, lo, these eighteen years, be loosed from this bond?

(Luke 13:16)

I spoke the letter **P**: *"Power of the Lord was present to heal them"* (Luke 5:17).

Q is also precious, honoring the mighty indwelling Holy Spirit: *"Quicken your mortal bodies by his Spirit that dwelleth in you"* (Romans 8:11).

The letter **R** signifies defeat for the Devil: *"Resist the devil, and he will flee from you"* (James 4:7). If we don't resist the Devil, he doesn't have to flee. But if we resist him, he must flee!

The letter **S** holds another expression of authority: *"Sent his word, and healed them"* (Psalm 107:20).

Here was **T**: *"Talk ye of all his wondrous works"* (Psalm 105:2). We talked of His works that night by Judy's bedside.

The letter **U** was next on this alphabet of healing: *"Unto you that fear my name shall the Sun of righteousness arise with healing in his wings"* (Malachi 4:2).

The letter **V** reveals Jesus' active ministry: *"Virtue* [went] *out of him, and healed them all"* (Luke 6:19).

The letter **W** is, perhaps, the Scripture we have spoken most often for healing: *"With his stripes we are healed"* (Isaiah 53:5).

I spoke the letter **X**: *"Expectation is from him"* (Psalm 62:5).

I assured Judy that the letter **Y** had been good for me for all these years, and it was hers to receive: *"Youth is renewed like the eagle's"* (Psalm 103:5).

I arrived at the final verse of this inspired alphabet, the letter **Z**: *"Zealous of spiritual gifts"* (1 Corinthians 14:12).

When I concluded speaking those twenty-six Bible verses over my daughter, I obeyed the Lord's Word to lay my hands on her for her healing. Then I had to leave the hospital.

My heart was filled with confidence that the mighty God was watching over His Word to perform it. (See Jeremiah 1:12.) No word from His mouth would return to Him void of fulfillment (see Isaiah 55:11), because God is not a man that He would lie to us. (See Numbers 23:19.)

The doctor said I could call the next morning. I called at 8:00 A.M. "Sorry Mr. Gossett, we have no information about your daughter to give you now. Call back in another hour," they told me.

I called again at 9:00 A.M. Again the response was the same. "We have no information to give you yet. Call back in another hour."

God watches over His Word to perform it.

At 10:00 A.M., I called again. The nurse responded, "Right now twelve doctors are surrounding your daughter's bed. But I have no information to give you. Don't call us again; we'll call you."

I waited patiently in my hotel room, pacing and praising God for the anticipated good report.

When the phone did ring, it was Dr. Clark. He said, "Mr. Gossett, this is remarkable. It's like we have had two different women in that bed. Last night when we took blood, results showed that the infection was severe. We gave her no medicine, because we didn't know how to medicate her.

"This morning we took blood again. Now her blood is completely clean and pure! We have just now discharged your daughter from this hospital. We will be putting her in a taxi for the trip to Heathrow Airport. She will be joining you for your flight back to America this afternoon!"

I was practically shouting praises to the Lord! I quickly packed my bag and checked out of the hotel. I boarded a bus to take me to Heathrow Airport, but in my excitement, I got on the wrong bus and had to get back off again. When I finally arrived at Heathrow, Judy was waiting for me!

If you need healing, I recommend that you affirm all twenty-six of the Bible verses listed in this chapter. They contain God's healing provisions for your spirit, soul, and body. Believe and receive your healing!

Afterword

|DEG|

I am watching to see that my word is fulfilled.
—Jeremiah 1:12 (NIV)

When our words are in agreement with God's Word, we experience the continual manifestation of God's blessing.

Here are just a few of the "word victories" I've known after walking with God by agreeing with God.

"Can two walk together, except they be agreed?" (Amos 3:3).

Only eighteen months after we lost a home by repossession, the Lord provided us a wonderful new home in Surrey.

The Lord put me on international radio, and the finances have come in, month after month, for more than forty years now.

The Lord removed a cancerous growth from my head just hours before my scheduled surgery.

When I was a lonely man after the death of Joyce, my dear first wife, in 1991, God brought sweet and delightful Debra to become my wife. Again, I must say, "Praise to the Lord" ten times!

The Lord led Whitaker House to begin publishing my books, eventually even translating them into many other languages.

After reading my book, *What You Say Is What You Get,* the men of World Harvesters in New Jersey invited me to be an evangelist for great crusades in India. More than two hundred thousand were reported "saved by grace through faith" (see Ephesians 2:8) in the first three crusades.

I was invited to preach to eighty-nine nations through Trans World Radio, originating from Monte Carlo, on a superpower station originally built for Hitler to proclaim Nazism.

God gave me total healing from violent headaches, climaxed by a personal visit from an angel of the Lord. Precious experience! That was in 1976, and I would be the most surprised person if I ever suffered from another headache after that Word victory.

To the best of my memory I have never, in fifty-three years, missed a preaching assignment because of ill health. By the grace of God, I never have to miss "life abundant" because of having to take a day off for sickness.

When my daughter, Judy, was stricken with a rare blood disease, the spoken Word caused the deadly sickness to vanish from her body, and her life was saved. Praise the Lord!

Words work wonders! Words that agree with God's Word will never return void.

My word...that goeth forth out of my mouth...shall not return unto me void, but it shall accomplish that which I please, and it shall prosper in the thing whereto I sent it. (Isaiah 55:11)

Faith Journal

Reaching and Touching in Faith

Don Gossett said his extreme financial need made him a "desperate man," causing him to seek God's ways to overcome the adversities, defeats, and bondages of his life. (See page 27.) Often we come to a place where we must acknowledge that only God can help us before we are ready to receive His provision.

Read Judges 7:1–15. How did Gideon reach out in faith and trust God for deliverance? When have you reached out in faith in the past? How did God bless your trust in Him?

Reaching out in faith results in the most significant touch of all—the touch of God.

That We Might Be Healed

Read the account of Christ's crucifixion in Matthew 27:32–54. Read Isaiah 53:5.

Before Christ's death on the cross, we were soul-sick. Worse than any cancer or disease that could harm our bodies, our souls were contaminated and putting us in danger of eternal death. Examine the health of your soul. Is your soul sick? Is your body ailing? Do you need healing? Does a friend need healing? Only faith is required in accordance with God's Word. Pray for healing for soul and body, and record your prayer below.

Daily Affirmations

Meditate on the Scriptures in this list of affirmations. (See pages 38–41.) Are these truths of God affirmed in your life? Why or why not?

After studying this list, add some affirmations of your own that apply to difficulties you are facing. Record them below.

An affirmation is a statement of truth you make firm by repetition.

The Power of Affirmations

What usually sets the tone for your day (e.g. television, radio, newspaper, other people, feelings of worry or being unprepared, the Bible, prayer)? How do you normally respond to negative thoughts from yourself, the enemy, or other people? We are called to testify to the truth. How are you affirming to your own soul what Christ has done for you and who you are in Him? Record your thoughts here.

The Believing Heart and the Confessing Mouth

Read Luke 1:26–38, 46–55; 2:8–19. As the mother of Christ, Mary had a powerful testimony. She exercised wisdom and obedience in sharing it when God led her to in the power of the Spirit. When she did share her testimony, it was to glorify God and not her own worth.

Do you give testimonies to pass along information, pat yourself on the back, or make people feel sorry for you, or do you aim to glorify God in all you say? Pray that your testimony would be a powerful witness to God's working in your life, rather than merely a chance to expound on your own abilities, thoughts, or complaints. Record your prayer here.

Our witness should flow from a heart filled with a desire to speak it because He has been so good to us.

The Power of Spoken Words

Read Romans 10:10, *"For with the heart man believeth unto righteousness; and with the mouth confession is made unto salvation."* Have you confessed Christ and received salvation? If so, what are you confessing with your daily words, thoughts, and actions? What is the penalty for wavering in your confession? Record your thoughts here.

"Gosh, Sir, Isn't God Wonderful?"

In the story of Johnny Lake that Don Gossett related, what did Johnny do for Cathy that helped bring about her healing? Why was Dr. Riley healed?

Amos 3:3 says, *"Can two walk together except they be agreed?"* and Proverbs 18:21 says, *"Death and life are in the power of the tongue: and they that love it shall eat the fruit thereof."* God speaks words of life. What are your words and actions saying? Are they in agreement with God's? Record your thoughts here.

Putting Your Best into Words

Dr. Kenyon spoke about two salesmen who sold the same product. (See pages 65–66.) One was successful, and the other was not. What is it about a person's words that convinces you they are speaking the truth?

Read James 3:5–12. Are your words uplifting to others? Why or why not? The verses in James show us how powerful our words are and how helpless we are to try to shape them into something good. Meditate on these verses, and then pray that God would be the master of your tongue and conform your words to His. Record your prayer here.

You can fill your words with anything you wish.

Ordering Our Conversations Aright

What does the word *confession* mean as it is used in this section? How are you using the following types of words in your conversations, and how can you improve?

Words of Confession of God's Word:

Words of Praise:

Words of Edification and Grace:

Words of Health:

Faith-Filled Words:

Words of Authority over Satan:

How much mightier are the words of our pens and of our mouths when our words are the Word of God!

Don't Shrink Back from Being Used by God

Do you base your confidence on your own ability to believe or on the power of the name of Jesus? Do you understand what God means in giving you the use of His name?

Read Acts 4:27–31, 33; 5:12. What resulted when the apostles prayed that God would work through the name of His Son Jesus?

Meditate on each of these affirmations. (See pages 72–75.) Write your thoughts on each, and apply them to specific circumstances in your life.

His name on my lips is the same as if Jesus were present and operating.

Loose Talking

Is your mind poisoned or pure? What kinds of words do you speak to others—words that bless or words that curse?

Read Romans 8:5–8 and Isaiah 55:9. According to the Bible, your mind is poisoned; it has been poisoned since the Fall. You must take on Christ's mind and leave your own behind in order to regain a pure mind—and therefore pure speech. Pray that you might have Christ's mind, and then think of some specific things you could tell family, friends, or fellow church members to build them up. Record your prayer and thoughts here.

"Don't Break Me with Words!"

Read Job 19:1–26. How did Job's friends use their words for evil? How did Job show that words can be used for good? Are your words to your fellow Christians like those of Zophar, Eliphaz, and Bildad? How can you make your words *"apples of gold in pictures of silver"* (Proverbs 25:11)?

As Dr. Kenyon suggests on page 81, think of something of great spiritual importance and then consider how you can best express it to others. Write your thoughts below.

How little we have appreciated the tremendous power of words.

Words Can Work Blunders

What type of trouble has your unruly tongue gotten you into? Are you guilty of a dual confession (see page 85)? How?

Read Psalm 19:14: *"Let the words of my mouth, and the meditation of my heart, be acceptable in thy sight, O Lord, my strength and my redeemer."* Add a personal prayer to this biblical one, and record it below.

With your words, you constantly paint a public picture of your inner self.

Just a Word of Warning

What kind of atmosphere have your words been creating? What can you say to encourage those you love and sustain them throughout the day? Consider carefully what words of hope and inspiration would mean the most to them.

Read James 3:3–5. Just like a small rudder steers a large ship and a bridle's bit steers even the biggest horse, your tongue steers your life and the lives of those who depend on you. How are you steering your life? Is God at the helm, or are you? Does your family feel that you have placed them in a safe harbor, or are you speaking words that place them in a storm?

Wailing and Failing Go Hand in Hand

Read Matthew 8:16. With only a word, Jesus drove out demons and healed the sick. It's not the quantity or force or volume of the words you speak, it's the God inspiring them who provides the power. What power is behind your words? Who is inspiring them—God or Satan?

Examine the list of death-dealing words that give Satan access to your life. (See pages 90–91.) Do any of them sound familiar? Have you been speaking them either out loud or to yourself? Are you speaking in faith each day, or are you speaking in fear?

When you speak death-dealing words, you give Satan permission to come into your life, into your affairs.

Be Humble or You Will Tumble

Read 2 Chronicles 26:1–21. Don Gossett did not allow his pride to be carried as far as Uzziah's, but both missed out on God's blessings because of their attitude of pride. Is there something in your life keeping you from God's blessing? Is your reaction to suffering similar to Don Gossett's initial self-pity, or do you immediately seek God in prayer for answers?

We Have Victory in Jesus' Name

God can overcome even the wind and snow. E. W. Kenyon related his first-hand experience of this.

Read Mark 4:35–41. Not only can God overcome the storms of nature, but he can also overcome the storms of life. What storms do you need God to calm in your life?

Pray that you would trust God to enable your feet to walk through the storms of life. Record your prayer below.

Boldly Say What God Says

Reread the story of Don Gossett's healing in Nazareth as well as 2 Corinthians 12:9.

What are the weaknesses in your life? How do you make it through the day—on your own strength or on God's?

Don Gossett trusted in God for healing, a much-needed car, and funds for his mission to Africa. Are you trusting in God's strength to *"supply all your need"* (Philippians 4:19)? What has God provided for you that you can be thankful for and testify to?

It is essential that you take the Lord's strength daily.

Centurion's Faith

Read 1 Chronicles 16:7–36 and 1 Thessalonians 5:16–18. With what kind of attitude do you approach God? Is it an attitude of thanksgiving for the things He has done and will do in your life? Do you give Him praise or just petitions? Have you been like the nine lepers who pleaded for help but did not thank Jesus, or are you like the one who returned to praise Him?

When we learn to speak the Word and not the problem, we are on the road to absolute victory.

By Your Words

Read Exodus 4:10–16; 14:13–14. Moses was not an eloquent speaker. In fact, he resisted God's call on his life because he did not feel his words were good enough. He failed to realize that it was not his words that mattered, but rather the power of God behind them. But God worked in Moses' life so that, by the time the Israelites were ready to leave Egypt, Moses had learned to rely on God's words. Moses had become a powerful speaker.

Are your words more like those of Moses in chapter 4 or 14 of Exodus? How can you learn to rely on God for your words? Why is it important to let God be the Power behind your words?

A majority of men have gotten their feet on the first rung of the ladder of success by words.

Speak the Word Only

Are you living with a disease—physical or spiritual—that you need healing from? Do you believe that God has that healing for you? Maybe it is a friend or family member who needs healing. Meditate on the verses in the alphabet of healing. Believe and receive.

Read Luke 5:17–25. This man had both his soul and his body healed because of his faith. Christ asked, "Which is easier?" but completed both. He can do the same for you. In the space below, confess your need for healing and the faith you have that it will be accomplished.

Additional Notes

About Don Gossett

For more than fifty years, Don Gossett has been serving the Lord through full-time ministry. Born again at the age of twelve, Don answered his call to the ministry just five years later, beginning by reaching out to his unsaved family members. In March of 1948, Don overcame his longtime fear of public speaking and began his ministry in earnest, preaching for two country Baptist churches in Oklahoma.

Don apprenticed with many well-known evangelists, beginning with William Freeman, one of America's leading healing evangelists during the late 1940s. He also spent time with T. L. Osborn, Jack Coe, and Raymond T. Richey.

Don has penned many works, particularly on the power of the spoken word and praise. His writings have been translated into almost twenty languages and have exceeded twenty-five million in worldwide distribution. His daily radio show, launched in 1961, has been broadcast worldwide.

Don has five children with his first wife, Joyce, who died in 1991. Don remarried in 1995 to Debra, who has joined him in his ministry.

About E. W. Kenyon

E W. Kenyon was born in Saratoga county, New York, but moved with his family to Amsterdam when he was in his teens. Kenyon studied at Amsterdam Academy, and at the age of nineteen, preached his first sermon in the Methodist church there.

He worked his way through school, attending various schools in New Hampshire as well as Emerson College of Oratory in Boston, Massachusetts.

Kenyon served as pastor of several churches in the New England states. At the age of thirty, he founded and was president of Bethel Bible Institute in Spencer, Massachusetts. (This school was later moved to Providence, Rhode Island and is known as Providence Bible Institute.) Through his ministry at Bethel, hundreds of young men and women were trained and ordained for the ministry.

After traveling throughout the Northeast preaching the gospel and seeing the salvation and healing of thousands, Kenyon moved to California, where he continued his evangelistic travels. He was pastor of a church in Los Angeles for several years and was one of the pioneers of radio work on the Pacific Coast.

In 1931 he moved to the Northwest, and for many years his morning broadcast, Kenyon's Church of the Air, was an inspiration and blessing to thousands. He also founded The New Covenant Baptist Church in Seattle and was its pastor for many years.

During the busy years of his ministry, he found time to write and publish fourteen books, as well as correspondence courses and tracts, and write hundreds of poems and songs. The work that he started has continued to bless untold thousands.

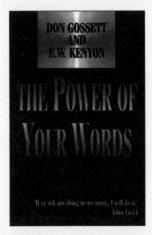

OTHER POWERFUL BOOKS

from Whitaker House

There's Dynamite in Praise
Don Gossett

Praise can bring life where there was death, freedom where there was bondage, and divine joy where there was sorrow. When you learn to praise God at all times and in all circumstances, you will experience a truly victorious life, and He will work wonders on your behalf. Discover the tremendous power that awaits you in learning to praise the Lord!

ISBN: 0-88368-644-9 • Trade • 128 pages

What You Say Is What You Get!
Don Gossett

Don Gossett reveals the power of words when we proclaim them in agreement with what the Word of God declares. His fresh and uplifting message of faith and hope will teach you how to receive healing, wisdom, answers to prayer, and much more. Discover the key to peace, love, joy, prosperity, happiness, and health as you become a powerhouse for God.

ISBN: 0-88368-066-1 • Pocket • 224 pages